Daddy's Money

For Jane –
Glad to meet you
in Kansas
City!
Yours,
Jo

Oct 2013

Also by Jo McDougall

Under an Arkansas Sky
Tavern Books, 2010

Satisfied with Havoc
Autumn House Press, 2004

Dirt
Autumn House Press, 2001

From Darkening Porches
University of Arkansas Press, 1996

Roots and Recognition
Pittsburg State University, 1994

Towns Facing Railroads
University of Arkansas Press, 1991

The Woman in the Next Booth
BkMk Press, 1987

Women Who Marry Houses
Coyote Love Press, 1983

Daddy's Money

A Memoir of Farm and Family

JO McDOUGALL

Foreword by Hilary Masters

The University of Arkansas Press
Fayetteville
2011

ISBN-10: 1-55728-967-0
ISBN-13: 978-1-55728-967-4

15 14 13 12 11   5 4 3 2 1

Designed by Liz Lester

☉ The paper used in this publication meets the minimum requirements
of the American National Standard for Permanence of Paper
for Printed Library Materials Z39.48-1984.

LIBRARY OF CONGRESS CATALOGING-IN-PUBLICATION DATA

McDougall, Jo.
Daddy's money : a memoir of farm and family / Jo McDougall ;
foreword by Hilary Masters.
p.   cm.
ISBN 978-1-55728-967-4 (pbk. : alk. paper)
1. McDougall, Jo. 2. Women poets, American—Biography.
3. Farm life—Arkansas.   I. Title.
PS3563.C3586Z46   2011
813'.54—dc22
[B]
2011021061

For Charles, who knows the time, the place, the people

For Duke and Lori

For Chris

and

in memory of my parents

Deciding to remember, and what to remember,
is how we decide who we are.

—ROBERT PINSKY

I read memoirs because I want to know how to live.

—ROBERT STEWART

the art of losing's not too hard to master
though it may look like (*Write* it!) like disaster.

—ELIZABETH BISHOP

Contents

Foreword

The shelf for the contemporary American memoir is increasingly occupied by accounts of incest and deprivation, drug and alcohol addiction, and grief. These narratives, nurtured as they are in sensational soil, almost always ripen into familiar success stories. Despite the horrors of an abject history, the subjects all come out okay. These personal testimonies are single-minded in their purpose to reveal the true grit of the memoirist with little reference to surrounding territory. Indeed, place, its ambience and effect, is given little attention and scarcely observed for its importance while the personal stuff of the memoir subsumes.

So it is refreshing to follow Jo McDougall growing up on her father's rice farm on the Grand Prairie of Arkansas, and to be made aware of the pulse of the gigantic Fairbanks pump as it watered the acreage, and to share her amazement and fear of the complex machinery of combines and threshers whose fast-moving belts could easily snatch away a hand or even a life. She observes these mechanical wonders as the phenomenon of her own being transforms her from girl into woman.

Work is a subtext of this memoir as it pictures the men and women who tended these fields and kept the homeplaces that represent and furnish this important corner of American history. McDougall reviews the final disbursement of these endeavors as her narrative describes the occasion of the auction that sells off the items of her history, piece by piece. Such is the fate of many farm families who have lived at the whim of the weather, and McDougall illuminates the pattern of her life with her family's history in a kind of pointillist assemblage. Closets are pulled apart, chests and bureaus are emptied, attics searched, and the odd corners of barns probed for artifacts and stories. The result provides the cause and effect of her own life as it gives a value to its habitat.

"Having set down," she writes, "the legends of a farm, a time, and my kin in this tribute to them, I know better now who my vanished predecessors were, the complex worlds they inhabited, the subtle ways they shaped me. . . . I found my way in this world alongside [them], and they proved to be sparkling companions. Over time, as with a painting left in the sun, their colors and outlines have faded, rumors of shapes where shapes had been. For me, however, they live in their fully faceted dimensions, no farther than my remembering."

A poet's memory gives this memoir its unique traverse.

—HILARY MASTERS

Acknowledgments

I thank the MacDowell Colony for residencies during the writing of this book, as well as Melanie Baden, executive director of the Museum of the Arkansas Grand Prairie, and Donna Robertson, administrative officer of the Arkansas Post National Memorial, for help in research.

Thanks to director Larry Malley and to my editors at the University of Arkansas Press, Tom Lavoie, Julie Watkins, Katy Henriksen, Brian King, and Carol Sickman-Garner, for their vision, attention to detail, and encouragement, and to Melissa King for her belief in the ongoing life of this book.

Deepest appreciation goes to my cousin Delano Black and his wife, Lynette, for their close editing, sharing of family archives, and translations. A very special thanks to Miller Williams, Hilary Masters, Andrea Hollander Budy, and Lewis Nordan, for their insightful, careful editing and wise counsel.

Thanks to James M. Duckett, Phillip McMath, Bryan Gammill, Conger Beasley, Bobby Ampezzan, William Trowbridge, Marcia Labrenz, and Donna Ziegenhorn for their input; to my cousins Melanie Gray, Edwin Lepine, and Antoinette Fenasse for sharing histories of the Lepine and Garot families; to Julie Amen for ongoing support; to Zada Simpson, Naomi Rousseau, Billy Gann Spratlin, Ellen West, Arkansas County judge Glenn (Sonny) Cox, Gordon S. Burnett, James B. Rasco, Terry Rasco, Sara Beth Dawson, and the many residents of DeWitt who contributed memories and anecdotes.

A loving thank you goes to my son, Duke McDougall, and his wife, Lori, for their untiring support and careful critiques. Thanks to my son-in-law, Chris Stone; to Cindy DeVasier; and to my grandchildren—

Tanner Stone, Shea Rivera, Lauren Bracken, Chandler Stone, Collin McDougall, and Merritt McDougall—for sharing their memories. And, foremost, to my husband, Charles—my gratitude, always, for believing in this work.

Grateful acknowledgment is made to the editors of the following publications in which excerpts from, and poems in, *Daddy's Money* first appeared or will appear:

Arkansas Review: "Excerpts from *Daddy's Money.*" April 2009, vol. 40, no. 1.

Arts & Letters: "In a Delta Courtroom They Settle the Estate." Fall 2005, no. 14.

Between Song and Story: Essays for the Twenty-first Century, ed. Sheryl St. Germain and Margaret Whitford: "Villa Augusta." Autumn House Press, July 2010.

Broadkill Review: "She Remembers a House." February 2010, vol. 4, no. 1. http://www.broadkillreview.com.

DeWitt Era Enterprise, sesquicentennial edition: portions of chapters 1 and 7 as "DeWitt Memories." October 2003.

From Darkening Porches: "The Suit." University of Arkansas Press, 1996.

Ghoti: "House." January 15, 2005. http://www.ghotimag.com/archives/issue1/mcdougall1.htm.

Little Balkans Review: "Where the Saltwater Can't Get at the Rice." Spring 2011.

mipoesias: "Summoning the Lost." Spring 2007. http://www.mipoesias.com/DAVIDTRINIDAD2/mcDougall_j.html.

Salamander: A Magazine for Poetry, Fiction, and Memoirs: chapter 2 and portions of chapter 1 as "from *Daddy's Money.*" 2005, vol. 10, no. 2.

Towns Facing Railroads: "Homeplace," "Small Town at Dusk." University of Arkansas Press, 1991.

The Woman in the Next Booth: "1942," "The Other Side." Reprinted by permission from BkMk Press, University of Missouri–Kansas City. 1987, 2002.

Author's Note

I grew up on a rice farm in southeastern Arkansas, near the small town of DeWitt, in a part of the Delta known as the Grand Prairie. I came of age during and immediately after World War II. *Daddy's Money* is the story of that time and place.

The catalyst for writing the memoir was my father's death, almost a decade following my mother's, and the subsequent settling of his estate. My sister and I were obliged to put our parents' assets in order.

Sifting through their belongings, I wondered who my parents really had been, how they had made their way. I wondered how that farm and town, my parents and grandparents and a whole quirky, compelling cast of characters, made me who I am.

This is an account of the struggle my grandparents and parents waged to be a part of the American story and to make a go of things. It's about farming rice—both as big business and as the day-to-day swirl of me and my kin who lived it. It's about the love of words that my mother, father, and a librarian in a one-room library during the Great Depression gave to me.

And in great measure, this story is about land—its vagaries and its grace, its lifetime hold on those who've lived upon it.

A word about the truth of things and the debate over memoir: Is it fact or fiction? Memory and story are powerfully intertwined; that's partly what makes us human. As writer John Barth has sagely commented about autobiography, "The story of your life is not your life. It is your story." I've tried to tell the stories true, in the spirit and texture of the voices, time, and places that shaped me, as close to the bone as I could get.

JO MCDOUGALL
2011

Map showing DeWitt and other sites of the author's childhood.

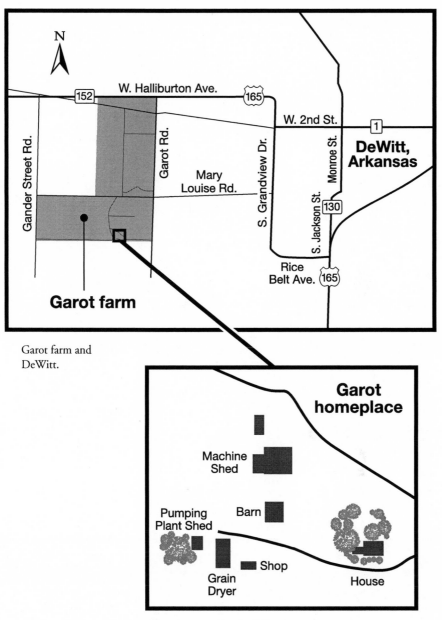

N

W. Halliburton Ave.

152   165

W. 2nd St.   1

Gander Street Rd.

Garot Rd.

Mary Louise Rd.

S. Grandview Dr.

Monroe St.

S. Jackson St.

DeWitt, Arkansas

130

Rice Belt Ave.   165

Garot farm

Garot farm and DeWitt.

Garot homeplace

Machine Shed

Pumping Plant Shed

Barn

Grain Dryer

Shop

House

Garot house and outbuildings.

Daddy's Money

SUMMONING THE LOST

I don't like writing about the dead,
conjuring them in language
that some of them
never would have used—
pushing them onstage,
saying, "Go. It doesn't have to be the truth."
Something's varnished about it,
all klieg lights and rouge,
all glistery shadows.
Yet what else is there to do?
Shouldn't you, Reader,
be led to see these glossy, passionate,
stumping souls
who once plowed a field in the teeth of a tornado,
waltzed with a wooden leg,
sashayed an armadillo on a leash?

Perhaps not. Perhaps you've
already left the page,
dealing with your own ghosts,
throwing them over your shoulder like salt:
a grandmother, a child,
a brother missing in action
who smoked every day a pack of Camels
and had a way with mules.

CHAPTER 1

Daddy's Money

MOTHER places one foot on the chicken's head and yanks. It flops a few feet in the stingy grass, blood spurting from its headless neck. I'm nine years old, standing in the drought-bitten yard beside my mother, learning how to murder a chicken: Hold it upside-down by the feet, put its head under your foot, and separate its head from its neck. Blood spatters Mother's shoes and cotton stockings. She doesn't seem to notice.

On this summer morning in 1944, my father herds his rusted pickup back and forth across the farm, checking a rice field or fixing a broken trac-tor part or feeding the cows. My sister, Nancy Ruth, my only sibling, is not yet born. The sun irons the moisture out of the sky, wilting the four-o'clocks and the cannas along the backyard's cement walk. My mother dis-patches three or four more chickens, then turns to me. "You do it," she says. "It's time you learned."

The chicken's severed head leans against my shoe, its eyes dum-founded. Chicken blood reproaches my bare legs. Mother murmurs her approval. "Good," she says. "But next time, make a quicker pull. You don't want to torture it."

In my growing up, there was an ample house, an elm to climb, a haystack, a barn, its smells of manure and wasting leather. Beyond the house, a Fairbanks Morse engine rose, tall as a church. It powered the well that pumped the water that grew the rice that made Daddy's money.

There was money there, as they say in the South. (Bordering Louisiana and Mississippi, the lower part of Arkansas is distinctly Southern.) But how much? Our father's estate, the source of bitter contention between my sister and me, escalating into litigation and roiling on for six sulphurous years, had been at various times valued as enormous, moderate, next to nothing. Who knew? Dad, who died in 1994, following my mother by nine years, was Howard Hughes–secretive about his holdings.

Daddy, the son of Belgian immigrants, was christened Leon Joseph Garot (correctly pronounced "Guh-*roe*" but Americanized to "*Gay*-roe"). He farmed rice, oats, and soybeans on Arkansas's Grand Prairie, a subregion of the Delta named for its Sargasso Sea of prairie grass, now essentially extinct. Grand Prairie dirt stretches flat as a countertop between the Arkansas and the White rivers. Our farm, eleven hundred acres, lay in the heart of it, some thirty miles from the legendary Mississippi River. We traded in DeWitt, a town some seventy-five miles southeast of Little Rock, the capital and center of the state. DeWitt's population numbered around twenty-five hundred in 1935, the year I was born.

Dad spoke no English when he entered first grade, and his French accent lingered on certain words all his life. Other characteristics set him apart in that small community. Despite prosperous times for farmers after World War II, my father dressed like a transplanted Abner Snopes, favoring coveralls, vinyl boots, and a greasy felt fedora summer and winter. He made a name for himself as a niggardly spender, an eccentric, an anachronism in an area where farming is a huge, corporate business.

Dad's frugality ruffled the local farm-implement salesmen, who hoped every planting or harvest to sell him a new plow, maybe even a tractor. Every year, he stonewalled them. "I'd bet everything I own that Leon Garot will never buy a new piece of equipment," complained one salesman— "not in my lifetime, not in my son's." My father prided himself on hanging on to everything, changing nothing. "There's nothing wrong with that tractor," he would say when my mother, exasperated from hearing complaints about repairs, suggested he replace it. "It's got another good ten years. You want us to end up in the poorhouse?" Afraid, I suppose, of being perceived as flaunting his wealth, he once bought a new, green Lincoln Continental and hid it in a machine shed for six months.

Despite his reputed stinginess—or perhaps because of it—my father bought one of the first self-propelled combines seen in the area, in 1944 or 1945. Excepting one other new combine purchased in his career, he never again was thus seduced.

———

Replacing the threshing machine, the self-propelled combine soon took over the Grand Prairie. Haughty and efficient, doing the work of dozens of men, it brushed aside the haystacks, the virile threshing crews, the weary horses and mules. After Dad adopted the combine, the hoboes Ino, Uno, and Dono—my father swore these were their given names— no longer materialized at our back door each September, expecting to work the harvest.

Harvest is, for most rice farmers, the payoff for indulging a temperamental crop for five or six months. One of the many demands made by rice is that it must stand in water for much of its growing season. Grand Prairie dirt, with its impervious hardpan clay beneath loamy topsoil, makes that possible. My paternal grandfather established himself on the Grand Prairie in the early 1900s, joining a wave of twentieth-century pioneers afflicted with "rice fever." Unwittingly, Granddad joined an industry that would eventually make Arkansas the number-one rice-producing state in the nation.

I grew up in the white, two-storied house Grandfather Garot completed in 1910 and later passed down, along with the farm, to my father. As did many farmers, my father prospered from food shortages in Europe caused by World War II; the house soon was remodeled into a low-budget version of Tara. My mother, christened Ruth Maurine Merritt, had no qualms about spending their newfound wealth, although she always demurred that we were "not rich, just comfortable." After the war, she arranged for new windows and sills upstairs and down, a sunroom, a four-columned front veranda, a white railing around the roof, custom-made draperies, and carpeting throughout the house. The change and expense brought my father nearly to tears.

———

In the course of settling Dad's estate, I considered the things my parents had amassed: land, woods, houses, stocks and bonds, sideboards, silver, diamonds, enameled boxes, keys. In the attic of that house I grew up in, I uncovered everything from camp stoves to baby beds—four generations revealing themselves, fanning out across the boards. Yet who were my parents, really? And their parents? And theirs? The aunts and uncles, the ragtag tangle of cousins?

I knew only a bare-bones history of my father's family: my grandfather Pierre (Peter) Joseph Garot came with his parents and six siblings to Louisiana from Charleroi, Belgium, in the mid-1800s, eventually moving north to Arkansas. Along the way, he married my Belgian grandmother, Augusta Josephine Fenasse, and succeeded, despite an unlikely beginning, as a rice grower.

I knew even less about my mother's folks. They too were farmers, of English and Irish stock. My mother's father, Jessie Butler Merritt, known as Butler, spent his nights as a security guard and his days on a tractor. He and my grandmother Hattie Edna (Harden) Merritt pinched a living from hardscrabble dirt, near the central Arkansas towns of Jacksonville and Cabot.

Now, sorting through my parents' belongings, I'd come head-on with the past and my kin—their skillets, their underwear, their rustling presences. Who they were and where they settled made me who I am. In my ancestry are joiners, coal miners, day laborers, surveyors, landlords, and most likely executioners ("Garot" is surely a derivative of *garrote*).

I wanted to know: What compelled my grandfather Garot to come to Arkansas? Did any of my ancestors fight in the Civil War? My father had told me that one of his aunts had spied for the Belgian resistance in World War I. Was it true?

I wanted to smell my mother's Blue Grass cologne again, unearth my father's shabby fedora. I devoured the brittle snapshots I came across in my ancestors' muddled possessions: Mother as a toddler on the Merritts' austere porch; my grandmother Garot in a beaver-trimmed coat beside a 1930s Chevrolet; Grandfather Merritt, frowning, posing me on his horse, Daisy; my sister pushing her doll stroller, taking the family dog for a ride. But how could I trace the conversations and intrigues, the undercurrents and crisscrossing paths? Everyone who could fill in the blanks was dead, or lost to me.

As I was growing up, Daddy's money had provided for college;

dresses from Gus Blass and M. M. Cohn—Little Rock's upscale stores; trips to Yellowstone, the Grand Canyon, and San Francisco. When I was twelve, we sailed on a banana freighter to Guatemala and Cuba.

Despite the fact that he drove his vehicles until they died, hoarded burlap bags and string, coaxed every last dollop of toothpaste from its tube, my father was, at least on paper, a man of means.

As the years spent settling the estate wore on, greed, mendacity, and sloth pared his wealth to a shadow. Then there wasn't much money there.

CHAPTER 2

Red Wagon

ON a sullen March morning in 1997, frost had set up house-keeping on the north sides of fence posts; the steely smell of sleet thinned the air. Mother had been dead twelve years, my father three. Recently retired from teaching at Pittsburg State University in Kansas, my husband and I had moved to Little Rock. My son, Duke, and I had come to the Garot homeplace to witness—as part of the process of settling the Garot estate—the auction of my father's farm implements, the contents of outbuildings and shops and sheds, the remnants of a farm, a life. My daughter, Charla Jo Stone, diagnosed in 1986 with melanoma and undergoing chemotherapy, had stayed at home.

Like chicks trailing a mother hen, the crowd—farmers, collectors, antique dealers, and the merely curious—followed the auctioneer to file inside my father's farm shop, once his unofficial office, where repairs had been made, the day planned, and orders given to the hired men. The diesel-oil smell of the dirt floor rose, undiluted, as if Dad had just opened the door and were walking to the vise. We stopped before a child's red, rusted wagon. Pulled from its customary place under the workbench, it languished, smaller than I remembered, most of its paint gone, missing two wheels. Yet it seemed to mesmerize everyone. A man standing beside me, an antiques dealer probably, overrode my every bid. Finally, perhaps sensing my anguish, he edged closer to me. "Was that your wagon?" I nodded. He stepped away. Then my sister, calling from the back of the crowd, bid an outrageous price, and the wagon was gone.

Of all the places on the farm, other than the farmhouse, my father's shop held the most meaning for me and probably for my children. Duke, Charla, and I had spent chunks of our childhoods there. My son and I stood silently as the auctioneer proceeded to sell the shop's contents. I heard Duke clear his throat as the ancient bellows, installed by my grandfather, went to a man from Iowa. The woodstove, the mallets and hammers, the pallets—all went. As we left the building, I noticed the remains of a raccoon, half skeleton, half leathery hide, caught in the rafters.

DeWitt Bank and Trust, recently named administrator-in-succession of my father's estate, had ordered the auction. Although named co-executrices in our father's will, Nancy and I, at my petition, had been removed by order of the probate court. For many reasons—most too personal, the details too tedious to belabor here—I realized as the estate unfolded that I couldn't work with my sister. However, being too far from central Arkansas and constrained by my teaching job, I didn't wish to act as sole executor; hence the appointment of the bank as administrator. Nancy and I had not spoken to each other except through attorneys in over two years.

The shop where my wagon had slept, like Rip Van Winkle, for almost a lifetime, posed an eyesore—small, cramped, plastered with yellow-brown brick siding. It had, however, enjoyed status as hub of the farm, and Bill Howe, my father's main hired hand, had reported here for work every day at six A.M. Bill—balding, blue eyed, and overweight—grudgingly indulged my whims, and I adored him. The summer I was five or six, we developed a ritual: I'd run to the shop after breakfast, pull out the wagon from under the bench, and beg Bill for a ride. "I've got work to do," he'd grumble. My father would agree, scowling at Bill. "I didn't hire you on for such foolishness." They'd both give in.

Daily, except for Sundays (my dad believed in the sanctity of the Sabbath), the path Bill and I took with the wagon proved exactly the same: to the house by way of the gas pump, one circle around the pump, two circles around it on the way back, a final short, breathless run over gravel to the door of the shop.

———

The auction had gotten off to a laconic start. Fanning out in groups of four or five in the farm lot, waiting for the auctioneer to arrive, some of the crowd had wandered into the farmhouse yard to stand under the one remaining elm, near the spot where I'd killed my first chicken. The men wore caps proclaiming *Ag-Pro* or *Case* or *John Deere* above the bills. Most were farmers—sons and grandsons of men who had known my father. Nancy and I had been away for decades. Had they not been expecting to see the heirs, almost nobody would have known us.

The men kicked at imaginary circles in the ground, talking about the weather, the market for rice and soybeans, the best place to hunt whatever was in season. A man and his wife had set up shop on the grounds, selling barbecue, coffee, and three kinds of pie—coconut, chocolate, and apple—from a flatbed truck. Business was lukewarm, at best. Near the end of the auction, the man instructed the auctioneer, "Sell the whole damned mess—the smoker, the truck, and what's left of them barbecue sandwiches."

A farmer himself, Duke knew most of these men. Not many, however, had seen him since the previous fall when, at the age of thirty-five, he'd been hit by a hemorrhagic stroke. The stroke had taken from him the use of his left arm and leg; he walked with the aid of a brace. Nevertheless, farming was Duke's world; he approached a group of men and shook their hands with his good hand as if nothing had happened.

At an estate auction, people don't like to bid against the heirs, and the auctioneer showed little zest for his work. The auction of the Leon J. Garot Farm Equipment and All Contents of Outbuildings Regardless of Condition had begun with lot #1, the listless, rain-ruined junk in the carport.

Junk, I'm sure, is how most people that day would have dismissed the paint-needy house (off-limits for the auction), the leaning sheds, the tired combines. The bank had wanted to move the equipment to Arkansas's legendary Back Gate sale, held at that time close by the juncture of the Arkansas and Mississippi rivers—but no one could persuade the old John Deeres and Farmalls to start.

Before the day was out, my son and I would see small pieces of our lives disappear—tool by tool, building by building, bid by bid. Our past would be loaded up, taken away by pickup or van or trailer truck: the anvil, the baby-chick feeders, Daddy's leaning-tower collection of paper sacks, the upright piano my mother had grown up with, abandoned to the lumber shed.

Like good pilgrims, Duke and I negotiated the obligatory stations, following the auctioneer to the storage shed, the money-green pickup in which I'd learned to drive, the bob truck with my grandfather's name, *P. J. Garot*, scarcely legible on the doors, the barn with its odds and ends of harness, a smell always of impending rain.

I'd had a party in this barn the day World War II ended, in 1945. I was not yet ten. My sister was not yet born. My girlfriends and I, none of whom had lost anyone close to us in the war, celebrated with Cokes and chocolate-chip cookies. From the loft, we could look down on the fields of rice, silent except for the crickets, waiting for harvest.

Agitated, tossing her purse on her mother's oak sideboard that's ensconced in our family room, Mother turns to my sister and me. She has come home late from a neighbor's sale-on-the-grounds. "Girls, I'm telling you. Whatever you do, don't ever sell my things at auction."

Everyone knows the story. Everyone has a tale of blood ties gone bad, of betrayal, avarice, deceit—and every story is unique and particular. In the case of Dad's estate, the struggle over rightful inheritance turned sister against sister, friend against friend. Each time Nancy and I faced each other in court, I thought of funerals—the ancient formalities, the soundless ticking of bodies and time. Only three miles from the DeWitt courthouse, my father's pastures slept, the farmhouse filled itself with the odor of long silence, and the sparrows threaded their samesong under the eaves.

By late afternoon, the sky turned gray and hard as slate. Soaked with cold, disheartened, Duke and I moved with the crowd into the old orchard where the last lot waited for the gavel. My father's lackluster cars, trucks, plows, and tractors had been lined up like field artillery. Duke surveyed the adjoining pasture. "When I was little," he confided, "I was scared of the cows." He grinned. "Granddaddy said I couldn't be a farmer and be scared of a cow."

Except for the quarrelsome departures, the settling of debts, and the loading up, the auction was over. I'd lost the one object I came for. Duke had bought nothing. "There were a few things I wanted to bid on," he said, "but I didn't have the heart." We headed for the car in a freezing drizzle. As if Duke and I were of no more consequence than beetles, my sister brushed past.

Of the dozens of trees my grandfather planted in this orchard—pear, persimmon, apple—only two pear trees have survived. My dog and I spent countless summers here, lying on the grass, wondering at clouds, mindful of wasps, doing nothing until my mother stepped out from her All-Electric kitchen, calling me to supper. I realized that, depending upon the distribution of the estate assets, I might not come here again.

Hauling the equipment to the orchard had caused deep ruts, making walking a chore. I offered Duke my arm. Christened Charles William McDougall III, named for his father and paternal grandfather, Duke has inherited and refined their amiable, uncomplaining ways. Smiling, touching my shoulder, he declined.

CHAPTER 3

A Footstool with Hooves

MY mother's attic offers no electricity. Darkness weasels in, even on this faultless November afternoon. The outer corners of the house bemoan the wind—which, I'd learned as a child, was a mystical woman flying over the landscape, her long hair cascading behind her. It's 1997, forty-two years after my marriage, and I've come to the attic looking for my wedding dress. I'm also looking for the stuffed dog I had as a child, the yellow one that smelled like pee.

Relics of the four generations who'd lived in the house suffer abandonment here. Dirt permeates my hands, my nails, my lungs. I can't get enough of it. I rifle through magazines, clothes, and boxes like a refugee after garbage. In my sixties at the time, I feel like a child again, daring a forbidden kingdom.

My son-in-law, Chris Stone, and his older son, Tanner, who's seventeen, have ventured into the attic with me. Duke has joined us for the trip but is waiting in the hallway below. Due to the stroke, it's difficult for him to climb the attic stairs.

Chris and I, sanctioned by DeWitt Bank and Trust to enter the house, ply our flashlights over the attic's rubble. The dedicated collector of the family, Chris shares my passion for old things. "Look at this camp stove!" he says. "And a lantern . . . and here's a water canteen. I wonder who used them. Wonder where they liked to camp . . ." Tanner calls down to his uncle Duke that he's found a toolbox complete with tools, "like new, almost."

The rooms below the attic brood, empty since the early 1990s. Their contents had been taken to my sister's property in Edgemont, on Greers Ferry Lake, after Daddy moved, due to ill health, to be near Nancy. Not much survives in the spaces below us: a single volume of *Encyclopedia Britannica*, three antiquated adding machines, a baby-grand piano nobody wants to move. The fragrant life of the house has dissolved—my mother in the kitchen, icing a sponge cake; my father at his desk, paying bills; my grandmother Garot in the dining room beside my grandfather's open casket, holding his hand.

Of the many who ate and laughed and slept here, only my sister and I remain. A little over ten years old when she was born in 1946, I was fascinated by this newborn. I also was afraid; Nancy was the first baby I'd been around. "Be nice to your sister," my father would regularly admonish. "Don't raise your voice." I didn't know then about my mother's miscarriage, that Nancy was the child my parents thought they'd never have.

There were perks, I soon discovered, to having a younger sister. Nancy brought variety and vibrancy to my life, and I liked helping her learn to bike and roller skate. I also enjoyed occasionally flaunting my elder status, demanding my preferred seat in the family Buick. When Nancy was seven, I fled for college, but as she entered high school, we grew close. As adults, we were confidantes. However, as the events of settling Dad's estate unfolded, I saw these bonds unraveling.

Entering the house this afternoon, I'd been accosted by its familiar smell of old papers, Christmas candles, and overripe bananas. With my parents gone, the odor falls sharper, too sweet, born of cold and dust. It loiters on my hands for days.

———————

In the attic, I've become my mother. Scenes from her life, real and imagined, scratch across my mind. Details of my childhood leap up like flame. I find my old rock collection; I thought Mother had thrown it out. Chris swings his flashlight close to the striped agate, aqua-colored crystal, and geodes collected from those ubiquitous roadside rock shops of the 1940s. On our family vacations, I clamored from the back seat for Dad to stop at every one.

The attic is a teeming place, and keys to how I became who I am present like puzzle pieces: Grandmother Garot's fashionable hat pins. A footstool made from the hooves and hide of the only deer my father ever killed. Photographs of my grandfather Garot's four sisters—Therese Marie Catherine, Leontine, Marie Catherine Gustavine, and Melanie Joseph—brunettes all, with hourglass figures. A pair of wooden shoes, souvenirs of the Netherlands. A pearl-buttoned house dress my mother had sewn on the battered Singer. My steamer trunk, its pennants cheering for Stephens College. My father's fraternity pin. Instructions for making a stand-up paper pig.

To my dismay, however, I don't find my wedding dress. Mother had stored it, keeping it for the granddaughter she hoped she'd have. After Charla chose not to wear the dress, I lost track of it. I'd like to pass it down to my granddaughters; I think the dress would bring them luck, as I had a magical wedding.

I met Charles W. McDougall Jr., the son of a rice farmer and a farmer himself from the neighboring town of Stuttgart, at a Methodist Youth Fellowship meeting in DeWitt. It was a smothering-hot summer evening. The meeting was held in the basement of our church.

During the social hour, I noticed Charles—tall (6'6", I would later find out), with red curly hair and a smile that could melt Antarctica. As the meeting was breaking up, he strolled over, introduced himself, and asked to take me home. I'd also noticed that he had brought a date. I declined.

Knowing he was too much the gentleman to leave a girl stranded, I asked him once what he would have done had I accepted. "Well," he said, "my date and I would just have taken you home."

Charles and I dated for four years. Sometimes moonlight sleeping on our street takes me back to those summer evenings when Charles took me home after a date, the windows of his green Ford coupe rolled down, the smell of low-hanging dust mingling with the smoke from his Lucky Strike.

We were married in 1955, in the church where we met. I wore the long white dress and misty veil I'd dreamed of years ago. I was nineteen, newly graduated from Stephens College, then a two-year college for women in Columbia, Missouri. Charles was twenty, in his junior year at the University of Arkansas–Fayetteville, the university system's flagship campus in the rugged Ozark Mountains.

Our wedding day in July was shingled with heat. Because the hordes of candles on the altar kept sputtering in the wake of the church's air-conditioning, Mother had it turned off. My grandfather Merritt took exception to this. "Dang it, Ruth," he groused to Mother at the reception, held at home, "I bought a brand-new suit with a vest for this, and now it's up and ruined."

The wedding photographer spirited us away from the reception in his Cadillac convertible. We sped to the nearby airstrip where Daddy had learned to fly, and a friend flew us in his Cessna to Memphis, where we began our honeymoon, destination Quebec City. After finishing our undergraduate degrees at the university, we came home to the McDougall farm near Stuttgart to raise rice.

This reads like a fairytale. By grace these things happened to me; I've no idea why.

I had hoped to present this storybook story to my granddaughters, Shea and Lauren, along with my wedding dress. It's nowhere to be found.

———

I continue to rummage Mother's attic. Coming upon my sister's toy stove and her old coloring books, I feel a twinge of sadness. Some three years ago, before we parted ways, I would have told Nancy about my findings, and we would have reminisced. Surrounded now by the artifacts of family, I feel the loss of not sharing the memories. Judging by my sister's recent hostile actions toward me, however, I realize this loss may not mean so much to her.

I'm looking for more than steamer trunks and hat pins and a wedding dress in this attic. I'm wondering how my mother and father made their way in the world, how I began making mine. Somewhere in this rubble lurk the clues.

Mother and Dad, doers as well as dreamers, forged a charging drive to succeed. They strove for financial security, for a standing in the community. They never said no when asked to volunteer. Whenever I was asked to teach Vacation Bible School or serve on a 4-H committee, my father would insist, "Don't turn it down. It's an honor they asked." He was first-generation American, glimmering with desire to be let in.

I find my high school report cards, signed by my father in his slanting, muddled scrawl. He ordained that Nancy and I make the highest grades. "What's this?" my father would ask me, pointing to an A- on my card. "Next time, it had better be an A."

To help me keep my grades up, Mother held spelling drills for me each night after supper during the school year. High expectations lived and had their being in my father's house: Be smart. Well-liked. Nice to everyone—almost everyone. DeWitt, small-town and Southern, could scarcely claim tolerance as its strong suit. Segregation and class distinction had long bedded down in the culture, intractable as the housefly.

Although as a child I didn't consider my parents racists, most probably would. They did laze along with the status quo. They disdained, while pretending to tolerate, blacks, as African Americans were called then. Mother, who in the early 1960s started Gallery G, an antiques and gift shop on the courthouse square, heard all the breaking news. When a car accident at nearby Dead Man's Corner killed three men one summer, beheading one, a customer brought Mother the news. Mother had a single question: "Black or white?" "Black," the woman answered. "Probably drunk," my mother concluded, turning back to her display of antique watches. In my childhood, I didn't hear of lynchings, but bodies of black men often were found floating in the bayous. Police investigations into causes of death were scant, if they took place at all.

Mother hired a black woman, Beulah, to clean house and do the ironing. A disheveled outhouse hunkered on the edge of our yard, overgrown with weeds, and Beulah was expected to use it. At noon, after my folks and I had eaten lunch, Beulah would sit at the table alone, eating from what was left. Troubled at this, I challenged my mother. "Why can't Beulah use our bathroom? Why can't she sit down at the table with us?" "It just isn't done," Mother would say. "Beulah would be uncomfortable. She wouldn't think of sitting down with us or using our toilet." How did Mother know, I wondered. I never heard her have a conversation with Beulah, other than explaining what she wanted done in the house. Mother explained: "Even if I gave Beulah 'privileges,' she wouldn't accept them." I began a protest, but Mother waved me away: "It just isn't done."

A large, billowing woman, Beulah leaned from side to side as she walked and smelled of Ivory soap. Somewhere she had learned the arcane, lovely art of packing a suitcase. When I went to summer camp with my clothes packed by Beulah, wrinkles never found a purchase in my blouses and shorts.

DeWitt's attitude toward strangers and each other alternated between biased and hateful, generous and warm. Families endured there for generations. Farmers' sons stayed home to farm, and farmers' daughters married them. Land and businesses passed down. It was a closed world, often cruel; gracious manners and egregious elitism shared equal billing. "Southern hospitality," a native Southerner once remarked to me, "is based on hostility." That paradox of love and manners, malevolence and guilt, makes the Southern psyche a snake's nest of contradictions.

The class system, although denied, prevailed, and I wasn't always courageous in trying to circumvent it. I remember with some self-reproach a girl in high school I'll call Alice Jean. Her father had vanished when she was a baby; she and her mother lived with the mother's alcoholic brother in a crestfallen house at the edge of town. Alice Jean walked to school no matter the weather. She lacked the requisite penny loafers or sweaters trimmed with Peter Pan collars. Smart, witty, with freckles and the aura of the defeated, she was shunned from any clique. For a brief time, I claimed her as a friend. She drowned in the White River shortly after graduating from high school. It distresses me to recall that, busy at college, I didn't come home for the funeral.

The subtleties of class, of social and financial arrival, concerned my parents. They were farmers; they worked the dirt, yet they had means. They signaled their station in life—solidly middle class—by choice of vehicles, housing, vacation spots, and dress. My father, who wore khakis and, occasionally, overalls to the field, dressed unfailingly for church in a dark suit, white shirt, and a tie secured with a silver, monogrammed tie clip. He bought property, usually sight unseen, in Texas, Florida, Jamaica, and Canada. Since most of it has proved near worthless, I conclude he bought it simply to be able to say he owned land "all over the place." No doubt he thought of it as a building block toward making his way.

When I was in grade school, Mother went door to door in town each Saturday, selling milk and eggs. With this pin money, as she called it, Mother, too, was making her way. It provided the extra cash necessary to expose my sister and me to DeWitt's cultural offerings. Diligently, Mother drove us into town for lessons of every stripe—voice, piano, elocution, tap dance—things she'd been denied. I took "expression" lessons, a low-rung form of acting, given by a decorous young woman in the front room of her house.

If fencing had been taught, we would have taken fencing. Or offset printing. Or the sitar. "Advantages," my mother would repeat like a mantra. "I want you girls to have advantages."

I had a room overlooking my father's fields and my mother's crape myrtles. Dad brought me motherless baby rabbits; there was always a dog. The radio nourished us, the four of us listening to our favorite heroes of the Sunday-night shows, Jack Benny and Fred Allen. When the radio proclaimed Franklin Delano Roosevelt's death, Dad summoned my mother. "Come here, Ruth. Listen." They sat wordless, stricken, staring at the dial as if they could make the president appear.

———

I bring my flashlight closer to a small tin trunk. "Ruth Merritt" is stenciled on its flat top. Chris and Tanner are chatting about the contents of an armoire, but silence roars so solidly that I hear nothing, neither their voices nor the wind nor a car on distant gravel, as I open a stack of letters tied with a shoestring. They're from my father to my mother, written in the months leading up to their August 1934 marriage.

I read greedily, too fast, my heart racing. I learn irresistible, mundane details. I read, for instance, that my father's parents and my mother called him "Garot." I never heard my mother call him that. When did she stop? Why? When did he stop calling her his "Ruthy"? My parents met when they were students at the University of Arkansas. He graduated in 1933 with a degree in agriculture, she in 1934 with a degree in home economics. The letters bridge that year when they were separated, living in different towns.

On May 10, 1934, my soon-to-be father writes his sweetheart, my future mother, from his job at the Rice Branch Experiment Station. A research component of the University of Arkansas's College of Agriculture and now named the University of Arkansas Rice and Research Center, the station lies between Stuttgart and Almyra. Dad describes a long but fulfilling day at the station. He's also enclosed an article from the *Arkansas Gazette* that outlines the perils newly married couples face in the

Depression. "Sweetheart," he writes, "I fear for us somewhat. . . . There is only one thing I wish to say: happiness means more than having many things, and if we are to wait until everything is favorable, that time will never come." He speaks of "being willing to start with the bare necessities," of "having faith," of determining to "work wholeheartedly for one another."

Dad has closed the letter with "Goodnight, Ruthy, Sweet [almost every sixth word in his letters is *sweet*], and hold me close . . . as we go to our dreamland." As I'm reading, I recall the first time I happened upon my parents' love letters: I found two or three in Mother's hope chest (like her jewelry box, off-limits to me) when I was twelve. Of course I read them with delicious guilt, astonished to find my parents had been passionate beings, but also reassured. If they loved each other, I had self-ishly reasoned, surely they loved me.

My mother was raised on the Cabot farm by a soft-spoken mother and a proud, independent father with Irish blood. The first of her family to attend college, she went by grace of student loans. "I had two dresses," she often recounted: "one for school, one for church." In contrast, my father's upbringing seemed luxurious. His family's prosperous rice acreage under-wrote his education; amazingly, he owned a car when he entered the university in the blighted year of 1929.

The attic presents the lives of my kin in chronological circles like the rings of a tree. In the farthest corners lie the relics of my great-grandmother Garot's early housekeeping: three battered side chairs, a ponderous iron chandelier with missing globes, the chimney for a kerosene lamp. In the next wave I find my grandmother Garot's yellowed silk blouses. Chris and Tanner find a white, flawless, ironstone basin. Boxes from my father's col-lege days, one housing letters from home and an Art Deco belt buckle, appear next. Then relics from my grandmother Merritt's house, brought here by my mother—a butter churn, a few giant gourds. Then Mother's Christmas decorations, most of them mouse-chewed beyond redemption. I report these to Duke, who remembers almost every ornament on Mother's Christmas trees.

I take a second look at the gourds. I remember that my grandmother

Merritt had used a hollowed, ivory-colored gourd to dip well water when she wanted a cool drink. It was at least 1950 before her household received plumbing. Upside-down under a moth-riddled rug, I find the slop jar my grandparents used at night to avoid trips to the outhouse. In over a decade of summer visits to my grandmother's house, I was asked to empty the jar only once. That was my grandfather's chore, dispatched each morning at sunup before he stumped to the field.

Almost to the end of her life, Grandmother Merritt tended to the major part of the cleaning, cooking, ironing, canning, and gardening. The chores never ended. She died of a stroke on a pummeling-hot June day, in her garden, toppling into a row of hollyhocks. My grandfather thought flowers a waste of good dirt. "Blast it, Hattie," he would storm, observing her rows of snapdragons and zinnias with petals the size of hippo teeth. "We can't eat petunias."

My mother's things are near the attic's pull-down stairs. Tanner and I sort through them. We find battered cookbooks and a well-thumbed manual for freezing corn. A trim five feet, five inches and 120 pounds when she married, Mother quickly put on weight. Perhaps it was the gnawing of the Great Depression, perhaps the example of her kin, but Mother lived to eat. On summer days, she canned regiments of tomatoes, snap beans, peaches, and black-eyed peas. When quick-freezing became the wave of the future, my mother embraced it. For weeks my father, sister, and I were regaled with her newfound passion. "First you blanch the corn," she'd say, her voice aglow with knowledge and wonder. "Then you can freeze it, right on the cob." A new Hotpoint freezer took up residence in the washhouse. When she died, there were three—overflowing, lids refusing to close over their bounty and sealed by frost. She had dated every package. Some chicken parts had lain there, stupefied, for twenty years.

Most of the freezers' contents came from the enormous garden behind the clothesline, next to the brooder houses. I hated it. It was home to garden spiders, slugs, and snakes. "Go pick what's ready of the purple-hulls," my mother would instruct on summer mornings, handing me a battered aluminum pan, "and check the pole beans." Even immediately after dawn, the garden fumed, hot and humid. When I stepped through the gate, clouds of mosquitoes covered me like black lace.

Snakes presented no problem: I carried a hoe for hacking off their heads. Garden spiders, on the other hand, sent me into paralytic fear. I had heard tales of an elderly cousin being spider-bitten, chunks of flesh falling from a hole in her arm that wouldn't heal. Once when I was five, running back and forth through sheets drying on the clothesline, I ran too fast and ended up full-speed at the garden fence, lunging into the web of a black and green spider that glistened as if shellacked. I can still feel the surprise of the web against my skin and see the spider, its trademark white zigzag in the center of the web.

Even though my husband and I farmed for twenty-five years, I never planted a garden. And I've never met a spider, large or small, that I don't despise.

————

In a pile of *Good Housekeeping* magazines near the attic stairs, I find a maroon spiral notebook. On its cheap ruled paper my mother set down, each Saturday night, her teaching outline for the Young Women's Methodist Sunday-school class. We knew to leave her alone in those moments, though the phrase "needing my space" hadn't yet been coined. I remember the silence, the rustling sound of her pen on paper like the wings of a wasp.

My mother was making her way. Uneasy about many things, especially her crimped background, she nevertheless was finding a distinctive place in her husband's church, in his community. In her class on Sunday mornings, my mother quoted from the gospels of Matthew or Luke. To that end, on Saturday evenings she turned away from the laundry, her family, and the stove to put to paper some loving, admonishing, careful words.

CHAPTER 4

Mother

SCOUGALE'S Fine Jewelers loomed in a corner of DeWitt's courthouse-square, its black-marble storefront sleek and formidable. Inside were tiled floors, brightly lit cases, and a cylinder of artificial flowers in colors not seen in nature. I was there under duress: Mother had decided it was time I chose a silver pattern. "That way," she reasoned, "people will know what to give you for graduation." I was a sophomore in high school; I had miles to go before graduation. I had no steady boyfriend, much less a prospective groom who would provide, it was hoped, the house to put the silver in. No matter—somewhere in my mother's mind lived a bible of Southern rituals with a chapter titled "Bringing Up Daughters" and "Thou shalt select thy silver early" one of its commandments.

Malcolm and Wilma Scougale owned the store. An outline of a huge diamond with sunburst rays beckoned from its hanging outdoor sign. Most folks in DeWitt eschewed such luxuries, but the Scougales were ever hopeful.

It was 1950: Eisenhower, crinoline skirts, Brando rising, *Father Knows Best*. Whether a girl had actual plans to marry right after graduation or not, it was assumed she would. Sooner or later, you'd better believe. Mother and the store proprietor began their campaign. "Why not start working on your silver right now?" Mrs. Scougale advised. This was a daunting goal—a project, like teaching Vacation Bible School both sessions, or tailoring a wool suit with bound buttonholes for 4-H, or earning a high-merit badge in Girl Scouts. (To my chagrin, I failed Girl Scouts. I fell in a creek on the first outing and quit the next day.)

Mrs. Scougale was a short, stout, decisive woman, one of those women in DeWitt who shaped my life, although I wasn't aware of it then. These women ran the shops, trolled through the gossip, influenced local politics, and helped mothers make decisions about their daughters' jewelry and silver and friends. Control was simply something they did, handed down by their elders, a grave and honorable duty. They did it effortlessly and with varying degrees of charm.

Armed with tradition, the store owner sat me down at a showcase rich with sets of silver flatware, dozens of them. The store smelled like the granite shoreline of Maine. Fluorescent lights blinked; the air-conditioning, newly installed, was set low enough to freeze a walrus. Everything in the store bristled with temptation, catering to every venal craving and desire. Black velvet purred in the showcases; small white boxes promised instant romance.

Mrs. Scougale was talking on, presenting one pattern after another. Traffic crept soundlessly, as if on snow, around the square. Behind me the courthouse sat stolid and unperturbed. In its upstairs library, Mrs. Miller was sorting books. "Frenchy" Trichell, in his repair shop down the street, was testing a percolator on the blink. Mrs. Bonner was dusting a display of hats. My father was somewhere in the heat and dust, walking levees, maybe, or tending a sick calf. "Your silver . . . ," Mrs. Scougale had intoned, the words hanging ephemeral in the air. I was walking down the church aisle in a long white satin dress, smiling mistily behind a lacy veil. I was Rita Hayworth, Ava Gardner, Hedy Lamarr. I would love Mrs. Scougale forever.

"Rose Point is what you want," my mother nudged. Years later I learned that Rose Point was one of the five top patterns Southern girls traditionally choose, a fact chronicled, no doubt, in Mother's bible. The rationale Mother gave that afternoon was that she owned a service for twelve in Rose Point crystal—sherbets, waters, iced-teas, wines—and my sister and I would inherit them. "Might as well match your silver to your crystal," she crooned. Mission accomplished.

Mother believed in using her good china and crystal, setting the table with it each Sunday that we ate at home. We ate in the dining room, using Grand Baroque silver flatware and Lenox china. It was my duty to set the table. "There's a right way and a wrong way," Mother instructed. "Forks to the left of the plates, knives to the right, with their rounded edges facing the plates. Then the spoons beside them." To this day, no matter how rushed I am, I can't set a table without putting the cutlery in the right order, seeing to it the knives keep their swollen edges nearest the plates.

Each girl who registered for silver flatware at Scougale's received a miniature silver spoon in her pattern, tricked out as a lapel pin. I thought wearing one's silver pattern on one's lapel pretentious, even tacky—tackiness being in my book synonymous with sin. I put the unworn spoon in a jewelry box that played, when opened, "Beautiful Dreamer."

The good folk of DeWitt did indeed give me pieces of Rose Point silver for graduation. Eventually, counting my wedding gifts a few years later, I assembled a service for twelve. I managed to acquire some of Mother's Rose Point crystal at one of the Garot estate auctions. Dealers bought the rest. The set had been Mother's pride. When did she buy it? Where? It seemed it was always there, brisk and flowery, the first of many sets of crystal that filled four china cabinets in the dining room. My children called that room the "ice palace." This pleased Mother, who now had the means and the know-how to accumulate the luxuries she'd never dreamed of in her father's house.

There were other coming-of-age rituals more against the grain than wearing a silver spoon, rituals over which Nancy and I had heated arguments with Mother: beauty pageants (Queen Mallard), cooking contests (Miss Fluffy Rice), and summer camp (Aldersgate, at that time not much more than a reclaimed turkey farm near Little Rock). Mother did her best to install us in all of them.

Choosing a college, however, escalated into warfare not unlike that at Gettysburg, Iwo Jima, or the Battle of the Bulge. Nancy and I each had graduated at the top of our class. We had scholarships; we also had strong wills. Mother wanted Nancy and me to attend Stephens College. A girls' school! I wanted to stay in Arkansas and attend Hendrix College, where many of my friends were headed, where there would be *boys*. "But Mother," I argued. "Meredith is going there, and LeRoy, and Bill, and . . ." I went to Stephens. A decade later, in 1963, when my sister graduated from high school, she vetoed Stephens, opting for New College in Florida. Mother was aghast. "Too liberal! No morals!" she stormed. Nancy did not enroll in New College.

I graduated from Stephens; Nancy went there a year. Then, because Mother thought that even Stephens was becoming immoral, she insisted that Nancy come home. My sister launched her campaign again: "New College," she seethed, setting her jaw. "Out of the question," my mother and father announced, glowering. They would not be moved. Nancy enrolled in the University of Arkansas at Little Rock, rented an apartment, and began her escalating alienation from Mother, whom she saw as a roadblock to glittering horizons.

Nancy was right; Mother and Dad were of the Establishment, firmly ensconced. When Haight-Ashbury came along, my father ranted endlessly about "those lost, skinny kids on drugs, sleeping in the street with filthy Communists and any other garbage they can drag up."

Everything my mother and father had dreamed of, scrimped for, and planned was threatened by the changing times. They'd mapped out Success in those long-ago love letters; they would not go gently into that 1960s night.

No doubt, Mother never understood her younger daughter. But who can unravel the treacheries of family? One decade and hundreds of miles from Nancy, I heard of the arguments between Mother and my sister; indeed, I often tried to arbitrate. I see now that subtle changes in power and allegiance must have occurred beyond my notice, collecting like sunlight on branches, shifting then disappearing.

Nancy's fractured relationship with me may have begun in those years when my sister found herself thwarted by Mother, whom I resemble in appearance and temperament. A decade older than Nancy, married with two children, a stay-at-home wife, I likely joined with the Establishment in Nancy's mind. Perhaps she transferred her resentment toward Mother to me, a situation exacerbated when she and I became jointly responsible for settling Dad's estate. I'll probably never know when the "first, slight swerving of the heart"—as Longfellow writes—took place and Nancy began to distance herself from me.

There was a time, nevertheless, when Nancy and I, each in our own way, shared the same goal: to get out from under our parents' roof. We had much intensity then, but little understanding. Caught up in our own Armageddons, we couldn't see what prompted Mother's obsessions, couldn't fathom that, in our mother's mind, her bulging closets held only two dresses; that the house she'd transformed into Tara had bald spots in the linoleum and smelled of sausage.

HOUSE

The house of my grandparents,
austere as an antler,
why did I love it?
with its needy porch and its yard dirt,
its one magnolia tree that never blossomed.

Butler and Hattie Merritt, my maternal grandparents, lived at the end of a take-your-sweet-time road with a low-water bridge. Their meager homestead in the rolling clay hills near Cabot became my home for a week every summer, from the time I was five until I was fifteen. Granddad Merritt grew a little cotton, but corn was the major crop. With its thin topsoil, his land wasn't suited for growing rice.

My grandparents gave me affection and freedom. I roamed outdoors for hours among the polka-dotted guinea hens, giving them unabashedly trite names: Cluck and Birdie and Peck. I told myself wondrous stories in my grandmother's garden, hidden by rows of pole beans, posing in front of the sweet peas. I wandered down to the creek, singing "Mairzy Doats" or "I Come to the Garden Alone." I contemplated the abyss of the rock-rimmed well, its dark water hauled up for drinking, its Paleolithic breath. I visited the ancient mule and the horse in the barn; I called the horse Salt although her name was Daisy.

My visits soon fell into a pattern. Mornings, I went with my grandfather on some adventure—a trip to Jacksonville or Cabot, or slopping the hogs. Granddad Merritt owned these eighty acres free and clear, every rod of which he had walked, the lay of the land rising through the soles of his feet. I thought it a privilege to head to the field with him to check a fence or the tasselling of the corn.

Afternoons, I dressed and undressed my Greer Garson paper dolls and answered questions from Grandmother about things at home. In the evenings, I sat on the open front porch with my grandparents, Aunt Alice (Granddad's sister), and—when he was home between marriages—Uncle Coy, my mother's brother.

On particularly muggy nights, Uncle Coy and Granddad would crank out homemade vanilla ice cream that I never liked but pretended to. I wanted the store-bought kind, smooth and creamy, with tutti-frutti. The porch ceiling was painted blue, as was everybody's—does anyone know why?—and in the yellow light of the naked bulb hanging from it, the blue turned a dispirited gray. Idle talk drifted up, inconsequential as smoke. We watched the one tree in the yard, a magnolia, lose its battle with the dark, then slowly, suddenly vanish.

———

"Watch that step, now." Granddaddy Merritt takes my suitcase. The starched ruffle of my pinafore brushes my cheek as I slip my hand into his, negotiating the last, highest riser into the house. I'm nine going on ten this July day in 1945, arriving for my customary visit. I'm slightly in awe of my grandfather. There's a protruding wen in the middle of his forehead and a pencil-line scar where a mule had kicked him when he was a boy.

"Jo! Darling!" I'm standing in the glassed-in sleeping porch that serves as a family room, though my grandparents never would have called it that. Grandmother bends to hug me. "How's your mother?" Grandmother's skin is paper, and she smells of talcum powder and Bengay. The room contains a bed, a leather "fainting" couch, my grandfather's platform rocker, and the console radio—a Philco even older than the one in my parents' living room and stern as a judge. The radio is silent, but I can smell the orange light of the dial, a waxy mix of dirt and wisdom, older than elephants or the Euphrates.

Grandmother has outfitted the bed I'll sleep on tonight—and all the beds in the house—with feed sacks bleached and sewn into sheets. The crocheted bedspreads boast elaborate patterns she's invented: Pinwheel, Sunbonnet, Moon over the Mountain. Every Tuesday, my grandmother starches and irons the bedclothes and airs the spreads on the clothesline beside the garden.

Grandmother Merritt has considerable needlework talents, which she aims to pass on to me. Each evening of my summer visits, at her bidding, I'll watch her embroider feed-sack sheets, pillowcases, and dish towels—any plain cotton surface that comes to hand. By the time I'm thirteen, she'll have taught me the tedious art of embroidering French knots. I'll take home a pair of pillowcases decorated with flowers, each with a tiny, silken knot in its center. Smugly, I'll present them to my mother, who'll store them in the linen closet, saving them for my hope chest.

The bed in the sleeping porch is cool and vast as a mesa. If it's too hot to play outside, I'll sprawl across it, reading or decoding old stains in the ceiling. Uncle Coy, who'll claim the couch for afternoon naps, will snore relentlessly, an oblivious, Niagara Falls noise. My grandparents, of course, will sleep in the "master" bedroom, another term no one in that house would have used. It smells faintly, darkly, of my grandfather's roll-your-own cigarettes. Sunlight seems reluctant to enter here. An odd uneasiness comes over me as I glance into their room. I make a silent vow never to step across its threshold.

"Come here, Honey." Aunt Alice holds out her arms, sagging with fat and disuse. She's calling me from her wheelchair in the kitchen. Aunt Alice and her daughter, Mollie, came to live in the Merritt household when Mollie was a baby. Mollie is like a sister to my mother, whom she calls "Sis." The whereabouts of Mollie's father, Mr. Legg, and the circumstances by which Aunt Alice and Mollie came to live here are never discussed. Until Mollie married Albert Andrews and left home, my grandfather had six mouths to feed plus the livestock. The corn crop never made enough money, and his job at the base was sporadic at best.

"Just look at you!" Aunt Alice exclaims. "I can't believe my goodness how much you've grown!" I let myself be drawn against her cotton dress with the V-necked lace collar, its bright, lifting odor of Garrett snuff. My mother abhors Aunt Alice's snuff-dipping habit, but I find it rebellious, delightful, and useful. Discarded snuff tins fit my collection of dead beetles perfectly.

The Merritt dining room, onto which almost every room in the house opens, is literally and spiritually the focus of the household. My grandparents eat breakfast in the kitchen but convene in the dining room for lunch and dinner—or dinner and supper, as they would say. Food is the overriding, guilty passion in this house, as it is in Mother's. Everything comes from the garden and the farm—great speckled lima beans, black-eyed peas, pork loin, cured ham, sweet corn, turnip greens, blackberries, and crook-neck squash. To humor my father whenever he visits, Grandmother will offer up a pan of overcooked rice, but the most care is lavished on the potatoes—mashed, whipped to a fare-thee-well, globs of butter on top like molten lava. I'm hoping we'll have this dish for supper tonight.

From persimmon jam to lime pickles, my grandmother cans everything, but it's the sausage patties that I do my best to avoid. They reside in her open pantry in clear glass Mason jars. Layered in beds of congealed grease, their round dingy eyes follow me everywhere.

There's no indoor plumbing; the outhouse is behind a privet hedge, and I've never mastered my fear of navigating the pathway to it, a series of skinny, rotten planks. For courage, I sing to the guinea hens and bantam roosters patrolling the grassless yard. Sometimes they croon back, mocking, their heads tilted, their feet thrust warily and painstakingly in front of them, like women in their Sunday shoes coming suddenly onto mud. I carry a stick for the wasps and pray not to fall into the dark hole that waits, miles deep, all-the-way-to-China deep, beneath the outhouse bench.

What lies beyond the outhouse, the barn, the hog pen, my grandfather's fields? Perhaps it's simply waiting—waiting to become a memory, like the next frame of a movie, there but not yet flickering.

———

On the way to the guest room, my very own for the week, Grandmother and I pass through the living room—or the front room, as it's known in this house. The smell of last winter's coals haunts the fireplace, aggressive and sad. Outside, under one of the windows, my grandmother has planted a few struggling rose bushes and hydrangeas, which she refers to as snow balls.

Opposite the fireplace stands the door to my room, with its bay window, twice-starched lace curtains, and iron bedstead. Grandmother leaves me to my unpacking. "You're all grown up now, Shortenin,' aren't you." Her voice softens. "I guess now you can do it all by yourself?" I hang up the sundresses, pinafores, blouses, and shorts my mother and the faithful Beulah have carefully folded, each item layered with tissue paper. In the closet I touch my grandmother's too-short, faded winter coat, Uncle Coy's government-issued greatcoat, my grandfather's rough, red-plaid mackinaw. These are their only winter clothes. The odor of mothballs eases into the room.

From the front window, I see my grandfather's fields sloping to the creek. "Tomorrow," I promise myself. Tomorrow I'll wade barefoot in clear water, smell the sun drilling into rock. The body of water nearest to my father's farm is a stagnant bayou, blanketed with green moss, home to turtles and cottonmouths.

I've just awakened in my Grandmother Merritt's house. It's December cold, the wind rattling the ill-fitting windows. The sun isn't up. I hear voices and laughter in the front room, a rustling at the fireplace. I peek around the door. My parents and my grandfather are filling stockings hung on the mantel—long, lumpy, cotton things I recognize as Grandmother's. It's Christmas Eve. There is no Santa, just my parents and Granddad filling ugly stockings with oranges and apples and last year's hard candy. The next morning, I pretend to believe.

Grandmother Merritt died in 1954, a year before my marriage. Uncle Coy lived a few years longer; my grandfather survived my grandmother by fifteen years. Some years after Grandmother's death, Granddad took another wife, a generous, pleasant, big-bosomed woman. Mother never forgave her for being in her mother's house.

My mother inherited the Merritt house and farm, selling it soon afterward. No one ever spoke of this. I wonder if the house still stands. I've never tried to find it. I imagine it, vanished except for its foundation, barely visible in the dirt, like teeth ground down. I envision the magnolia gone, the barn, the outhouse, the zinnias. There's nothing there. I'm treading a dream.

Among my mother's things I find a photograph of that house before I came to know it, when it boasted Victorian gingerbread under the eaves. On the porch, in front of the bay window of the room that was always mine, a child stands awkwardly, pigeon-toed, in a white dress and black stockings. This is my mother, her parents' great pride, the daughter and the scholar who minded her manners and brightened their world.

Grandmother and Mother wrote each other at least once a week until my grandmother's death. My grandparents had no phone, and we saw them only three or four times a year. Grandmother wrote on coarse, lined paper, sometimes in pencil, sometimes in ink, sometimes on penny postcards.

Grandmother Merritt's life was financially crimped, always. She grievously felt the pinch of it, especially in the matter of giving gifts. She writes a letter to Mother postmarked August 7, 1945—my mother's thirty-fourth birthday and one day after America dropped the atomic bomb on Hiroshima. (No mention is made of this.) Grandmother writes to apologize to Mother for not sending a present and to say she's had a canning accident. Mother worried constantly over the state of her mother's finances and her health, lamenting the distance between Cabot and DeWitt.

> Dearest Sis,
>
> Happy birthday to you. I'm sorry you couldn't be with us today. Mollie, Coy, and Gladys [Coy's second wife] said to tell you we enjoyed your birthday dinner. Had fried chicken, peas, & so on.
>
> Am sorry my card will be a little late but I couldn't get it any earlier. Am also sorry that I don't have any other gift for you but I think you will understand and I promise to make up for it some time. I scalded my foot pretty bad. Was scalding tomatoes to can.

The lid fell off the kettle and just all poured on my foot and filled my shoe. I couldn't even kick it off. Aunt Alice had to pull it off for me. It's almost well now but it sure did hurt. Otherwise we are well as usual.

Love,
Mother

The Merritt finances were especially strained concerning Mother's tuition and clothes for the university. In the spring semester of Mother's junior year, Grandmother writes about some dresses she's mailed.

May 20, 1933

Dearest Ruth,

Your letter came today was so good to hear from you also to know that you could wear the dresses, but am sorry the little blue one was so like the other one. . . . [It] didn't cost a fortune so if you want it keep it . . . I think you will find it practical and serviceable. . . . I am sending a dress that Mollie gave you. . . . I did the best I could with it. . . .

Well, write soon and don't worry about exams too much and I guess you can go ahead and make arrangements for the summer term—seems to bad to turn back with the end in sight. . . .

Lovingly,
Mother

It's late afternoon on this first day of my visit to my grandparents. I've hung up my clothes, visited Daisy, and pestered my grandfather to go into Cabot, to no avail. Grandmother and Aunt Alice are bustling in the kitchen, preparing supper. Yes, we will have whipped potatoes with butter and cream gravy, and No, there's nothing I can do to help, "not just now." I wander out to the porch. Uncle Coy lolls in a rocker and invites me to sit in the porch swing. It needs oil.

"What's that story about, Uncle Coy?" I ask, pointing to the book in his lap. "What's *Forever Amber*?" My uncle looks up, startled. I guess he's forgotten that I can read. He tells me I'm "too young to hear about that kind of stuff," closes the book with a snap, and goes inside. He never brings the book out in my company again, and I never find it, although I rummage everywhere.

Uncle Coy was overweight, subdued, a chronically disappointed man given to stomach ailments, dominated by his father. He helped out sporadically on the farm, tried several jobs in Cabot and Jacksonville, joined the army, and, briefly, was a sheriff's deputy. To Mother's dismay, her brother married and divorced three times.

When Coy died, Mother gave me his Masonic ring and the wedding band given him by Gladys. I've seen a snapshot of my uncle and Gladys on their wedding day. It's probably sometime in 1944, toward the end of World War II. He's in his army uniform. She wears a suit with a peplum jacket and a hat with a veil, tilted at a sassy angle. A breeze lifts the hem of her skirt above her knees. She has Betty Grable legs.

———————

"If you want to go with me in the morning, Bug, you better get up early, five o'clock, rise and shine," my grandfather announces, rolling a cigarette. My grandparents, Aunt Alice, Uncle Coy, and I have done serious damage to the snowy potatoes and fried pork chops, and we've gathered on the porch. "Five o'clock," Granddad says again. I look at my grandmother. Yes, she nods; she'll wake me. "I'll have to feed Daisy," Granddad says, "and then we might go see Mollie and Albert." Mollie and Albert live in North Little Rock, where Albert owns a furniture store. Granddad knows how fond I am of these cousins, their orderly house on Main Street, and the coconut cake Mollie likely will serve.

"I'll be ready," I tell my grandfather. I want to ride beside him in the old Chevrolet, feel the frizzy velour of the seat against my bare legs, and listen as he tells me who lives along the graveled roads leading to Highway 5 and North Little Rock. I want to be at the table when he eats his breakfast after chores—thick ham, tall biscuits, and red-eye gravy.

My grandfather's breakfast never varied, whether he stayed home or went to his second job as watchman at "the base," meaning the nearby air force base at Jacksonville. If he was going to the base, he'd mutter, "Put some of that ham in my lunch pail, Hattie. And don't forget the gravy. I gotta go." Tomorrow, however, he won't carry his lunch. Tomorrow, if we go to North Little Rock—and I'm certain we will—Granddad will take Mollie a tow sack of field corn or a mess of turnip greens. She'll cook lunch for us as she catches up on the Merritt news from my grandfather, shaking her head sadly when the talk turns to Coy.

———

"Diphtheria," my grandfather says, pronouncing it "diptheria." We're standing in the yard beside the Chevrolet just after sunup, ready to leave for North Little Rock.

Although no one has told me, somehow I know—as children always know those things adults try to keep from them—that my grandparents have lost twin boys, that the babies had been only months old when they died. But how did it happen?

Grandad removes the wide-brimmed straw hat he wears against the heat. He pinches the crown. "Diptheria," he says again. "The doctor came too late." He runs the backside of his hand hard along the hat's crease. "Your grandmother never got over it." A guinea calls, strident beyond the privet. Granddad opens the driver's side of the car, glancing toward the house. "You ask too many questions," he says. "Let's go." He turns the key in the ignition. Two crows fly out from the magnolia, scolding.

My mother led a harsh life in her parents' house. She hoed cotton, milked the only cow, helped with the canning. She ironed her father's and brother's khakis and uniforms, mopped the uneven floors. No electricity graced the house. There was the work, the meals served on oilcloth, the frugal, exhausted words, the kerosene lamps, smoke climbing their glass chimneys, the upright piano no one could play. I try to imagine the silence, interrupted only by crickets and owls, sometimes a rain.

CHAPTER 5

Pensacola

WHENEVER my parents argued—and as I came into adolescence, their arguments were frequent and intense—my father often would remind Mother how far she had come, how he had taken her from that "red clay farm" where she "had to pick cotton dawn to dusk" and "go to an outhouse to piss."

Mother almost never responded verbally to those cuts. Instead, whenever Dad threw her impoverished upbringing down like a gauntlet, my mother would storm out of the room. The next day I might find her prone on the family-room sofa, the curtains tightly shut against the Delta light, which could sack a room. "Hi, Honey," she'd murmur, reaching out one arm to me from under the crocheted coverlet. "Could you do the dishes? I've got a nauseating headache. It's probably a migraine."

The argument I remember most vividly occurred on a trip to Florida; I was probably six. Daddy had decided the family should get off the farm and visit the Everglades. On one of our nights on the road, we stayed near Pensacola in a typical 1940s tourist court—a flock of small cottages, each with an attached open garage. A free-standing office beckoned near the highway, "Vacancy" announced in blinking neon. I slept on a cot brought in by the owner's wife. I woke up in the night to my mother's strident voice berating my father—wasn't this the thousandth time?—for the dirt road they lived on, for not moving to town, for subjecting her to "dust, nothing but dust."

"Turn the light out, Ruth," my father demanded. "No," she answered, her voice icy as moonlight on a tin roof. "No, Leon. I'm going to read." Daddy leaned over Mother and snapped off the bedside lamp, a squat brown-and-turquoise thing, its shade the color of putrid lemonade. Silence roared like the inside of a conch. Mother began to cry. I pretended to be asleep. Then Dad got up from the bed, slammed as hard as he could the door with the pull-down shade, and disappeared into the Florida night. The door frame seemed to have misaligned itself with his fury.

I wanted to say something to my mother. I felt guilty, somehow responsible for this argument, but I said nothing. When Daddy returned, I squeezed my eyes shut, relieved and terrified.

Although I witnessed many of Mother and Dad's arguments over the years, I never doubted that they loved each other. After all, I'd seen their love letters, the ones I'd stumbled upon when I was twelve, snooping in Mother's hope chest. So why did they fight? I would ask myself, lying in the darkness of my second-story room, their rough voices racing up, mauling the stairs.

Sometimes the arguments started after supper. If it happened to be summer, I would walk out of the kitchen into the night, beyond the back porch, their voices scalding my back. Light from the kitchen washed onto the yard; beyond that was darkest dark, the stars where they should be, but wobbling. Sometimes my father would come to stand beside me, saying little, putting a hand on my shoulder as if to reassure me I was loved. Still, I would never feel more lonely. What had I done to cause these wars?

In a black-and-white Kodak snapshot, my mother and father stand in the side yard of the farmhouse, in front of a generous fig tree. They are newly married, unsmiling, 1930s Southern Gothic. Mother wears a white suit, probably linen, a small-brimmed hat angled over her short, marcelled hair. Daddy is in a shirt and tie and light-colored trousers, his suit coat momentarily discarded, due, perhaps, to the heat. The photo doesn't show that my mother had light brown hair and hazel eyes. Nor does it record the color of my father's eyes, brown as a deer's, or the even, olive color of his skin.

The house in the background, the one to which he has brought his bride, is Daddy's boyhood home, bearing still some touches of the Victorian. The furniture inside it is his mother's. When I was ten or so, when Mother arranged for the remodeling of the house, she dismissed her mother-in-law's furniture to the attic and outbuildings and hid the hardwood floors with carpeting: 100 percent wool and wall-to-wall.

———————

"She's late. She's always late," my mother fumes, referring to my grand-mother Garot. "She waits to go to the bathroom until just when I call her to supper." Even after making the house completely her own, Mother resented her mother-in-law's visits. Having retired with Granddad to Lake Hamilton near Hot Springs, Grandmother Garot continued to live there after Grandfather died.

On those visits to our house, Grandmother and Dad would often con-verse in French, much to the vexation of my mother. When Grandmother dallied, late to meals, Mother would start slamming things. I, on the other hand, relished my grandmother's visits, listening to her read aloud from the Bible in her rhythmic accent, taking in the lavender, salty smell of her room.

Even after my mother remodeled and redecorated, acquiring all the appointments of silver and china and cut glass the house could swallow, she continued in her campaign to move to town. She wanted out of the stuff of which my days and nights and dreams were made: sounds of mosquitoes, killdeer, and tree frogs. Endless fields. Honeysuckle and orange, aching moons.

"Dust," Mother hounded my father endlessly. "Dust and mosquitoes. I despise them." Our house was an easy three-mile drive from town, partly on macadam, partly on a dirt road straight as a broom handle. Indeed, the dust did spew behind the car in vaulting rooster tails. It settled on every-thing in the house, invited in, before air-conditioning, by the attic fan. Even after the house was outfitted with window air-conditioners in the mid-1950s, allowing us to close the doors and windows, dust found us. In spring and summer, battalions of mosquitoes sauntered through the finest of fine mesh screens.

My father would respond to Mother's haranguing that he was not about to live in town, that she had, after all, married a farmer. "For God's sake, Ruth! You knew what I was when you married me," he would storm. He reminded her that she had a "damned good life." If she'd wanted the "trimmed-grass, nine-to-five, know-what-every-day-will-bring-you" kind of life, my father shouted, she should have married that "weasel" she'd dated before him, "a dentist, for Chrissake."

Mother must have sensed that her cause was doomed. My father, devoted to his mother, bound to the memory of his father, kept everything on the farm exactly as it had been in his father's day, allowing only for enough improvements to make a decent crop. In those days of the 1950s, average yields per acre were fifty to sixty bushels of rice and twenty bushels of soybeans. My father contented himself with the average. By this time he had inherited the farm; having no mortgage payments and keeping his overhead low, Dad could concentrate on other interests that rivaled farming—tinkering, inventing, and the Democratic Party.

Dad's belief in absolute non-change colored all he did. When Grandmother Garot died, the house in Hot Springs remained, by decree of my father, as it had been the day she went to the hospital for the final time. Every magazine and medicine bottle was left precisely where she had placed it. The family used the house for a few years after Grandmother Garot's death, but we dared not open the kitchen or bathroom cabinets—who knew what we might find? Mother finally persuaded Dad to move his mother's furniture to the farm, before thieves "got everything." As the moving men came in, she reported, my father wept.

————

When Mother and Dad met at the university, she lived in the 4-H house and Dad in the Ag House, a fraternity for farm boys and agriculture majors. She'd transferred from Arkansas Tech–Russellville with her wardrobe of two dresses. The fact that my father had a car spoke of the economic disparity between them. "I'll try to get you some money next week," my grandmother writes to Mother in the spring of 1933, "but if you need any more after that, too bad." Despite this difference in their backgrounds, the tall, lean man and slender, smiling woman who would become my father and mother fell in love. It was 1932. Arkansas was in the dregs of the Depression, but they would marry. They had a plan.

In their letters, the roles my mother and father would each play in marriage begin to jell. My father appears fearful for their future, insecure. My mother bolsters him, encourages, reasons. "I cannot believe, Sweet," she writes to my father in 1933, a year before their wedding, "that we have made a mistake. . . . We have loved each other for so long. . . . I believe in you. . . . I've watched you meet all your obligations and never shun your duty. I trust you with all my life and heart." My father warns that, starting out, they may need to practice grating frugality. To this my mother declares, "I know we may feel that we are living in the simplest of necessities, but just to live wholly for each other all through the different ages of our lives is my constant prayer. . . . I don't ask for so very much, only to be with you." They made promises to "live wholeheartedly for each other." My future parents are determined to make a go of farming, parenting, and a life based in community, work, and the Methodist Church.

Of course, the marriage struck a few rocks. In Mother's hope chest, which sits now at the foot of my bed, I found a note tucked between molting sweaters. Dad has dated it 1944; they've been married ten years. He's written a somewhat pedestrian sentiment on an enclosure card from the Charles S. Stifft Co., Little Rock's leading jewelers at the time. I surmise it came with a conciliatory gift.

October 1944

Dear Ruth:
　　After ten years I look back and perhaps you are to be commended for your tolerance.
　　I hope that this may be a token of my appreciation of you and your efforts. . . .

Lovingly,
Leon

Mother had a deep-seated fear of water, which my father made little effort to alleviate. She balked at taking the ferry across the Arkansas River when we headed south for vacations. One of her cousins had drowned when his car slid off a ferry, but Dad ignored Mother's agitated protests, pressing on toward the ferry landing in the dark, saying nothing to her pleas to "at least wait till daylight to cross." She refused to ride in my father's motorboat when he took it out on Lake Hamilton. For this he constantly ridiculed her, comparing Mother to Aunt Alice, who, he said, "worried for a living."

My parents' marriage lasted, differences notwithstanding, until

Mother died—fifty-one years. Without her, Daddy was devastated, as he often said—pronouncing it de-*vas*-tated, still hearing the French inflection. He had lost his best friend. He adored her, seeing always, I believe, the young, struggling woman who earnestly became his bride.

———

Whatever faults Daddy may have found in his wife, lack of hard work surely wasn't one. Mother made good use of what she'd learned with her home economics degree to keep her household running evenly.

Home economics as a major was not for the fainthearted. Its candidates took inorganic and organic chemistry, often finding themselves in classes with pre-med students. Biology, zoology, and courses in nutrition were required, as well as hours in art, psychology, and child development. Majors also endured a stint in the on-campus Home Management House. Here Mother refined the intricate disciplines of making a home. She learned how to run a household on a budget, decorate the rooms, calculate the nutritional value of meals, name and describe hundreds of textiles. She could bake a perfect custard and tailor a man's suit. She steeped herself in the development of infants and children. She was consumer-wise. Like a great many women before World War II and Rosie the Riveter, Mother considered homemaking a venerable career.

Mother had already learned, of course, the practical household arts from her mother. In her own home, although she systematically acquired appliances to make life easier, Mother often resorted to my grandmother Merritt's ways. She hung the laundry on the line whenever she could, bypassing the willing G.E. dryer. She draped the throw rugs over the clothesline and beat them to remove the dust, leaving the staunch and upright Hoover to its closet. She starched and ironed everything, including the sheets and pillowcases. She grew a voluminous garden. She canned, filling row after row of pantry shelves with purple-hulled and English peas, lima beans and cut corn. To supply the three freezers, she scoured Arkansas's roadside stands, bringing home endless flats of Judsonia strawberries, bushel after bushel of Clarksville peaches.

To her credit, despite the fact that she employed Beulah, my mother determined that her daughters be taught to do for themselves. By the time we each had entered high school, Nancy and I had learned to change beds, do laundry, cook, clean, sew, bake, and murder chickens.

Mother's determination derived, no doubt, from the work ethic she'd learned at home. Grandmother's letters to us almost always included an account of her household activities. A letter she wrote in the fall of 1945 contains news of dressmaking patterns and soldiers returning home from World War II. She hints at a scarcity of goods in the stores.

November 28, 1945

Dearest Ruth, Leon, and Jo,

Received your letter today. Was glad to hear from you. We are O.K. except Dad has a cold. He hasn't worked in over a week but plans to try it tonite. He is on that graveyard shift. That in itself is enough to make him sick. And it's so terribly dusty.

We cooked our dinner Sunday and went to Mollie's. Think she and Albert both enjoyed it. . . . Dad dug our potatoes yesterday. They were surely fine. Got my gas heater in Saturday . . . but I just don't get anything done in the way of sewing. Seems like something is always happening.

Certainly wish it would rain. I haven't washed [clothes] this week. Water is so low. I have been canning some more. Canned 3 qts. of shelled beans, 6 qts. of butter beans, 4 qts. of tomatoes, and some tomato juice.

Marion is home on furlough. He came and had dinner with us yesterday. Parker got home too. Hughbert is all ready in the States and Turrell & Reginald are both home so they will all soon be home and I think they are a lucky bunch none of them got seriously hurt. Guess you seen by the paper about Nell's baby girl.

Haven't seen Coy and Gladys for some time. Uncle Jim is sick again and Uncle Will too. And the worst of all Eva is back like she used to be so I've heard, but I sure don't want to see her.

Ruth I hope you mean that about Xmas. For we sure can't hunt things even if they could be found. Every one tells me that things are scarcer than they were during the War. I think I'll just get a bunch of cards and you do the same.

Am sending you this apron pattern but you won't want to make more than one for they are a job. All those little petals have to be double and blind stitched down. Too much trouble for me. . . .

Don't know if I will get it together or not. We have butchered some since you were here. Still have 2 more, don't know just when we will kill them.

Give my love to Jo and Leon and you write soon.

Love,
Mother

Doing the family wash, referred to in Grandmother's letter, was a weekly, Sisyphean chore. It had to be done outside the house, rain or shine; huge iron pots had to be lined up for washing, rinsing, and bleaching with homemade lye. I remember my grandmother stirring boiling starch with a long wooden paddle.

At home, it was my duty to help Mother with the laundry, referred to as simply "the wash." We spent the designated day—usually Monday—in an all-purpose, tin-roofed building, the wash shed. It doubled as a dumping ground for storage and a place to incubate baby chicks.

Mother had advanced by that time to a Maytag washer/wringer, an engineering marvel: instead of wringing wet clothes by hand to ready them for line drying, one now could feed them through two joined, electrically powered, noisy and flexible cylinders reminiscent of rolling pins. I expected to see my fingers flattened thin as pie crust, like the shirts and sheets I sacrificed to the wringer.

The smells of starch and laundry soap and the steady groans of the Maytag served as touchstones in my world. Mother hummed some Irish tune or another, and I was secure, necessary to the scheme of things. Mother, the Maytag, and I were a team, engaged in a portentous ritual.

Mother's sporadic attempts at saving money often proved unsettling and unpredictable. A stainless-steel container sat on Mother's stove. After every breakfast, she poured bacon drippings into a stainless-steel container, substituting the grease for Crisco when making coconut or jam cakes. The combined taste of sugar and rancid bacon was rattling. Dad and Nancy and I protested. "Nonsense," she'd sniff, unflappable. "It's your imagination. You can't tell the difference."

———

Despite her carping at my father, despite her excellent record in household management—which, subconsciously, she may have thought would further her cause—Mother never succeeded in getting her house in town. In a closet of the farmhouse after Dad's death, I found blueprints labeled "Leon J. Garot Home." Probably my father commissioned them in an attempt to vanquish the escalating arguments, to stanch the wounds of Pensacola. The new house would have been ambitious and costly; I doubt he ever intended to build it. Perhaps he told Mother they'd put it on the lot in DeWitt that he later divided for rent houses. Perhaps he told her they'd build it on the farm, in place of the house that must have seemed to my mother always to belong to another time, another woman.

CHAPTER 6

Against My Skin

I'VE just arrived in New Hampshire from Little Rock for a second residency at the MacDowell Colony, a retreat near Peterborough for writers, composers, architects, and artists. It's May 1998, and I've taken early retirement from Pittsburg State, where I taught English and creative writing. My father has been dead four years.

During my stay, I'll be working on a poetry manuscript. After a four-year absence, I'm pleased to find the Adirondack chairs still angled invitingly under the cedars and the resident cat as I remembered him, enormous and sassy from table scraps and serious attention.

Legend has it that Thornton Wilder wrote *Our Town* at MacDowell, the oldest of the U.S. artist colonies. Leonard Bernstein, Aaron Copland, and Edwin Arlington Robinson live among the spirits glinting in every studio, on narrow paths, in the shadows of the four hundred or more acres of woods. On my first visit to the colony, I suspected benign ghosts had laid claim to my studio—the composer Amy Beach, perhaps, or Bernstein himself—delighting in the grand piano, black and glossy as patent leather.

I've drawn a different studio this time—large, speckled with sunlight, a veranda in back and tree-sized hydrangeas flanking its entrance. I'm grateful for the solitude, the wind, the one-note birds; the years since Daddy's death in 1994 have spiraled into a maelstrom. The Garot estate stands light years from being settled, and my sister and I are estranged.

In the few months that Nancy and I served as executrices of Dad's estate, we had numerous arguments—verily, conflagrations—as to its management. We argued bitterly, too, about Mother's jewelry and the fact that Nancy refused to show it to me, much less divide it between us, although legally this could have been done before settlement of the estate. Things quickly went awry, taking a course I found to be emotionally and financially harmful, one I couldn't sanction. Although I'm some fifteen hundred miles from Arkansas, I can't leave this story. It permeates my skin like perfume.

At my table for supper in Colony Hall, a converted barn, sit five fellow colonists, most from New York City, all younger than I by at least two decades. I compliment a woman to my left on the dress she's wearing—vintage 1940s, cap-sleeved with a flared skirt, colorful macaws tangled in its green background. The dress leads to conversation about vintage jewelry, and I tell her how I long to own something of my mother's. "It's been thirteen years since my mother died," I comment, surprising myself, "and I have nothing that was hers. Nothing. I want just one piece of her jewelry to hold against my skin."

At this, conversation at the table halts. My words float like corks. I might as well have said that I'd just seen the colony director running nude past the dining-room window. From across the table, a woman looks up. "I heard you say something about your mother's jewelry. . . . I've been talking real estate prices in Brooklyn, but now . . ." A composer at the end of the table puts down his fork. "I think it's a Southern thing," he says. "They're so into family there."

The colonists at my table have some notion a South exists; they just don't know where. "Arkansas," someone says thoughtfully. "Does it border Mexico?" "Close to Baltimore?" another ventures. "Can you get there from New York?" They urge me to continue the tale. I tell them some of the story, one that is indeed Southern, yet universal, biblical, and bizarre.

I tell them how my father had, after my mother's death, forbidden my sister and me to touch so much as a spool of thread in the house we'd grown up in, how he'd created a shrine to Mother—everything in the farmhouse they'd lived in for fifty-one years intact: sofas, shirts, Dutch ovens, Kleenexes in my mother's handbags. At her death, Mother had left not only her personal belongings but also her shop, Gallery G, to my father. Daddy decreed that nothing be touched there, either—not the contents of the vault nor the matched pair of Sevres vases nor the cheap music boxes with melodies like falling tin. "Now," I say, "my father is dead, and still I have nothing of my mother's."

At ground zero of the bitterness between Nancy and me lies the casket jewelry, the pieces Mother most favored, that she wore for the visitation. She was resplendent, adorned with her wedding-ring set, diamond cross, and a gold medallion engraved with the dates of her marriage and its fiftieth anniversary.

These special pieces, sources of joy for my mother, now rise sour and contentious. I want the pieces divided without further delay; I feel time dusting up its wings. Charla has been coping with melanoma for twelve years, and it has metastasized. I want to give her something of her grandmother's jewelry, now.

Eventually the probate court intervened. Less than a year before my daughter died in 1999, I received my share of the jewelry, giving some of it to Charla and some to Duke. For myself, I kept the golden-anniversary medallion engraved with a jeweled quarter-moon and star—something of Mother's, at last, to wear against my skin.

———

It took six grinding years, but Dad's estate was finally settled in 2000, year of the predicted apocalypse. The bulk of the estate consisted of farmland in southern Arkansas; the farmhouse; hunting land; the cottage on Lake Hamilton; the land in Texas, Florida, Canada, and Jamaica; cars; farm vehicles; farm equipment in various stages of disrepair; and the vast array of antiques with which my mother had filled the gift shop and the house. Besides the casket jewelry, there were other desirable pieces, such as a handmade, hinged silver bracelet Mother brought home from Guatemala. When I was in high school, I begged to wear it. I coveted, too, a vintage Navajo silver necklace; when I was six or seven, Mother had caught me wearing it as I pilfered her jewelry box. Mother's jewelry had mesmerized me: the pinched smell of tarnished silver, the rainbows erupting inside diamonds, the abrupt coolness of jade. The collection vanished after Dad's death, and Nancy and I quarreled repeatedly over this. I never discovered the jewelry's whereabouts.

After taking over management of the estate, the bank held a series of auctions in which my sister and I, the only participants, bid against each other for our mother's things. Thus I obtained a few of her belongings, but much of what I treasured in my mother's house eluded me, including my daughter's favorite doll.

On a few occasions, Charla—possessing always a mischievous talent for adventure—and I would embark on sleuthing (what Charla called "pinkering") expeditions. We hoped to locate any of Mother's silver, jewelry, or furniture that hadn't been accounted for, that might have been consigned or sold to antique shops in neighboring states. These were exotic, albeit not fruitful trips, seeing top-of-the-line shops and inventory but never spotting anything identifiable as Mother's. Giving up on our quest one day near Greenville, Mississippi, we decided to assuage our disappointment at Doe's Eat Place, entering through its fabled screen door embellished with a rusting *Holsom-Is-Good-Bread* sign, and ordering platter-sized steaks and house-made hot tamales.

My parents had accumulated, almost obsessively, countless treasures. What had compelled them? I wanted to know. As settlement of the estate dragged on, I wondered more and more about those who had come before me, who had given me such a grounded, secure, and brimming life.

———

Dad, Charles and I, Nancy, and Gus, her longtime partner, sit in the dining room of the Raphael Hotel in Kansas City's famed Country Club Plaza. It's late November 1990; Mother's been dead five years. At dusk, the plaza's Seville-inspired buildings hum with Christmas lights. The music dances, the candles come alive. Nancy and I chat. Gus, chiropractor and nutritionist by trade, bon vivant by choice, tells a story. We laugh louder and louder. A few couples at nearby tables turn to stare. "Some people just can't stand to see folks have a good time," Gus declares and orders another glass of pinot noir.

By the time Daddy died, I had shared with Gus and Nancy almost all my fears and hopes, despairs and joys. Together my sister and I had lived through challenges with my children and her stepchildren, career adjustments, illnesses, financial meltdowns, and triumphs.

I can't pinpoint when this close relationship began to fray, but after Daddy's death, a distancing began, almost imperceptible at first, then hard to ignore. I would plan to meet with Nancy; the meeting would be ignored. "I was too busy," she might say when asked why she hadn't at least phoned. "I've got an estate to run."

The final showdown between my sister and me occurred in Edgemont, in December, six months after Daddy's death. Hoping to reconcile with Nancy, I suggested that we appoint a third party as administrator and that we step down. "Otherwise," I said, "we'll be speaking only through lawyers." After much discussion, deciding that our relationship was too important to further jeopardize, we agreed: we would ask a third person to take over. Or so I thought. At dinner that night, Nancy vowed the opposite: "I have no intention of ever stepping down," she said. "I can't believe you fell for it." "And what about our relationship?" I asked. I don't recall an answer.

It's December 20, 1994. Had my father been alive, he'd have celebrated his birthday the next day. I meet Nancy at the First National Bank of DeWitt, where Dad had held his accounts, to deal with estate business. After our Come-to-Jesus argument the night before, neither of us wants to see the other.

For this appointment with the bank president, my sister and I wear dark, tailored suits and high-heeled pumps. To the young woman greeting us at the reception desk, we surely must look like eccentric dowagers, older even than her mother. She speaks in the way of many young women in the South, declarative sentences ending in question marks, like birch strips peeling from the tree. The officer we need to see, she says, is "with a customer." She motions for us to sit. "I'm sorry, Miss Nancy, Miss Jo—it'll be just a few minutes."

I glance at my sister. She's crossed her legs, swinging the left one quickly, repeatedly. We have an appointment. Our father was respected here, serving on the bank's board. Furthermore, we see nary a customer in the banker's open office. "What's this all about?" I say, looking straight ahead. "I'm sure I don't know," Nancy retorts. "Probably comeuppance." "For what?" "It's a bank," she shrugs. "Who knows?"

After seeing the bank officer, Nancy and I meet with the estate's attorney. We discuss the fate of Gallery G. I want to close it; it's hemorrhaging estate money. Nancy wants to keep it open. There is a vitriolic argument. "Don't do this, girls," the attorney admonishes. "Your mother and father—I knew them both—wouldn't have wanted this."

"Girls." I'm fifty-nine; Nancy is forty-nine. The word lingers in the air, a symbol of the way things stack up in small Southern towns. If an argument between two heirs, both mature women, can be reduced to a cat fight between "girls," problems with the estate can be marginalized. Gender makes a difference, too, in the way the heirs proceed. Once, after hearing of yet another argument between me and my sister, my accountant remarked, "If the two of you were brothers, this estate would have been settled a long time ago behind the woodshed."

As a younger sister, Nancy assumed all the nuisance roles little sisters are supposed to play. While Charles and I were dating, Nancy, at the age of five or six, was especially good at spying when Charles brought me home after a date. Sitting in Mother's living room on the hair-shirt Victorian sofa, we'd catch Nancy peering around a corner, her brown eyes sparkling and audacious. Charles would smile and offer her a quarter to leave the room. When Charles and I married in 1955, Nancy was my junior bridesmaid.

———

Shortly before Christmas of 1994, my inheritance in jeopardy and the differences with my sister seemingly irreparable, I decide to petition the probate court to remove Nancy and me as executrices. About to enter the tangle of litigation, I enlist an accountant and a lawyer. I'll meet in Little Rock with them at least once a month for the next five years.

A genial man with silvery hair and a disarming laugh, Carl Lacy, my accountant, championed my battle for my inheritance. Carl's Little Rock office spies on a wooded green space, a respite from commerce. Through the tinted glass, in spring and early summer, the leaves shone as if veneered with mirrors. By the time we went to court in July of 1995, they had withered like Dorothy's wicked witch.

———

After Nancy and I left the estate attorney's office that calamitous December morning in 1994, I parked in front of DeWitt's domino parlor on the square. With its pool tables and beer, this was a DeWitt institution I'd never entered. Bonner's Millinery, where Mother bought Easter outfits for Nancy and me, dozed down the street. DeWitt's weekly newspaper, the

DeWitt Era-Enterprise, kept its usual vigilance. Three miles away sat the farmhouse, taken hostage by mice.

I decide to visit Mother's shop, sitting across the street from the domino parlor. When Charles and I lived on the McDougall farm, Gallery G became my haven. Located only twelve miles from the farm, the shop resides in a vacated bank building, completed just before the Crash of 1929. In summer, its marble floors and thick walls protected me from the marauding heat. In winter, the furnace balked, and we might as well have been atop Mount Everest.

Established after I'd gone to college, the shop had been my mother's pride. The smell of dozens of perfumed candles overtakes me, and the years wind backward. I see Mother at her desk behind the jewelry counter, papers piled, unopened boxes stacked askew. "You can't sell from an empty wagon," Mother always maintained. Overflowing clutter forces me to turn sideways now through the aisles.

The woman running the shop—I'll call her Miss B—has been there for decades. Icily, she offers me assistance. (I'm sure she's aware that I want the shop closed, and probably she fears for her job.) I tell her I'd like to take a look downstairs, where Mother had stashed primitive antiques and collectibles.

"Help yourself," Miss B says. "But you'll probably run into your mother's ghost."

Grudgingly, she introduces me to an antiques dealer browsing in the shop; he appears to be in his sixties. He stops inspecting a piece of art glass and steps forward. "You're one of Mrs. Garot's daughters?" I agree to this assumption. He has a shop in northwest Arkansas, he explains. "I knew your mother for years. Fine dealer. Wonderful woman," he declares. He clears his throat and straightens his cheap tie. "I've seen the ghost. I wouldn't go down there if I were you."

"Ludicrous," I think to myself and descend the stairs. There's very little light in the room, it's damp, and shadows dart in and out of corners. I don't believe in ghosts, of course, but . . . I examine a few wooden-handled cooking forks, a churn, and a few oak chairs. I'm suddenly very angry. Who is that simpering man upstairs anyway? And why am I being made to feel like an intruder in my own mother's store? Settling my father's estate has become akin to finding myself in a Grade B movie, where everyone has been given their lines except me.

———

The abiding fascination of Gallery G lay in its two-story vault. A source of myth and mystery in the family, it opened with an elaborate combination Mother shared with no one except, perhaps, my father. Nancy and I knew the vault housed fine jewelry and silver, but what else? We could only guess. Mother rarely invited us into the vault, and a phalanx of boxes prevented our advance of more than two or three feet. My mother often commented that the antique silver stockpiled there, after decades of collecting, acted as her "insurance." I looked upon the vault with foreboding. I feared that one day Mother, having walked into it, would grow careless, and the great door would swing soundlessly, emphatically shut.

———

"What did you find in the vault?" I asked Nancy, excitedly, shortly after Daddy died, when my sister and I were, I thought, on good terms. Nancy had decided to clean out the vault, and I couldn't wait to hear of its bounty. "There isn't much there," Nancy replied with a shrug. "The silver's disintegrated, and the jewelry's gone. I'll bet Dad gave the jewelry to a girlfriend." Southerners buried their silver during the Civil War, I thought to myself. It doesn't disintegrate. And although Dad had a few women friends after Mother died, some of them family friends, it wasn't his nature to bedeck them with gifts. Looking back, trying to understand when Nancy's evasions concerning full disclosure of the estate began, I see the vault incident as an early clue.

By the time I enlisted James M. (Jim) Duckett as my counsel, in the last week of 1994, Charla had undergone the first of many surgeries for the cancer, and my teaching at the university teetered from my absences. In two years my son would suffer his stroke. With my life in ongoing chaos, I came to rely on the calm efficiency of my attorney's office: Jim always in coat, tie, and crisp white shirt, his desk in pristine order, the papers squared, a fresh legal pad and Mont Blanc pen before him.

Jim was patient with my near-zero knowledge of the law. "Well, I mean . . . ," he would say whenever I asked a naive question and then guide me through the legalese. Over the years, I learned how deeply he believes in the judicial system, how little patience he has for incompetence and deceit. I learned he grew up above a filling station in Wabbaseka and indulges a passion for model trains.

———

On a glass shelf in her kitchen window, my daughter kept a framed snap-shot of her aunt Nancy on a fishing trip. Charla and two of her four chil-dren, twin girls, stand in the foreground, their backs to the camera. Nancy helps one of the girls—she is nine or ten—with her line. A dealer in estate jewelry, my sister wears a few of her own signature pieces. It's summertime; the trees bend over the stream. The day captured here counts as one of many that my daughter's children, and my son's, spent with Nancy. She was their Auntie Mame.

IN A DELTA COURTROOM THEY SETTLE THE ESTATE

Like hyenas catching the scent,
the descendents gather to maul the carcass:
stocks, bonds, fields, owed rent,
the Midas flesh of their father.

It's tense in Jim Duckett's conference room. We're on the thirteenth floor of the Stephens Building in downtown Little Rock. It is 1995, early spring. In preparation for my petition to the probate court, Jim and I, Nancy, her attorney, and the estate's attorney have gathered. Because I feel that estate money has been spent carelessly in the estate office Nancy is running, Jim will take depositions from some of the office workers.

The conference table gleams, made of massive, solid mahogany. With wide expanses of glass on two sides, the room offers a giddy view of the Arkansas River, the I-30 bridge, and Little Rock's abundant trees. Less than a two-hour drive from Little Rock, Daddy's farm rests, absent of human life except for the men who rent it, absent of cows.

As the employees file in for their depositions, I feel as if I'm in the middle of a surreal movie. Nancy and I pointedly avoid each other. She has refined the art of the glacial stare; I haven't quite mastered it. I am suddenly, overwhelmingly tired. The room, the table, the river take on a gray sheen. Minutes earlier, as Jim and I entered the conference room, the husband of one of the estate employees berated us for, as he put it, "causing my wife and me to miss work, come all this way, and wait around just so two spoiled women can squabble at our expense." Jim was conciliatory. "I understand," he told the man, "but one day you may be fighting for your rights, like my client. Then you'll need somebody to weigh in for you."

There are more depositions to come. In June, Nancy, Jim Duckett, and I meet in the Conway office of Nancy's attorney. It's within walking distance of Toad Suck Plaza, site of the much-lauded toad races during the annual Toad Suck Daze. We're here for depositions; Nancy and I are to be questioned in anticipation of an upcoming court date. Each lawyer wants to know what the other's client knows that might prove harmful in court.

I'm nervous as Nancy's attorney questions me, Nancy sighing condescendingly with my every remark. After a time, Jim calls for a recess. In private, he tells me, jutting out his jaw and fixing me with his take-no-prisoners stare, "You're not doing well. Answer the questions courteously, but show some grit."

In retrospect, I think that Jim hit upon a key to the problems between Nancy and me. I'm not a confrontational person, and although Nancy was well aware of my misgivings over her handling of the estate, I suspect she never thought I'd pose a challenge. I don't know the motives for her near disregard for me as equal heir, but my nature, as well as the fact that I lived an eight-hour drive from central Arkansas, surely made me a less than formidable adversary.

As I leave Conway for Kansas that afternoon, my throat aches. By the time I reach Pittsburg, I have laryngitis. After numerous unconscionable delays, a court date is set in July for consideration of my petition.

———

When I step out of the car in front of the DeWitt courthouse on court day, the heat, hovering at one hundred degrees, drapes itself around me like a drunk wanting to dance. In a few minutes, I'll face my sister before a judge.

I've seen the courtroom only once, in the mid-1940s, when I was nine or ten; my father had decided I needed to know where city and county justice was meted out. Perhaps oblivious to the irony, he walked me past the *Colored* and *White* signs hanging above the water fountains, up the wooden stairs to the courtroom. The room, empty and solemn, seemed bigger than the Methodist church sanctuary and my school auditorium put together. I felt the presentiment of doom. I was afraid then, as I am now. Then I was a spectator; now I'm a player.

I take my seat in the courtroom beside my attorney, at a desk facing the judge's bench. The room glares at me as if embarrassed by its shabbiness. With its weary, flesh-colored walls and its dun-colored draperies, it exudes all the warmth of a New York City morgue.

The afternoon light glorifies a scuffed spot on the table where Jim and I sit. Mindful of what Daddy's money has bought and what it cannot buy, I think how close to—and how far from—I am to all I loved as a child. Then Jim is on his feet, making his opening remarks to the judge. We win this day in court; the judge orders Nancy and me to step down and names DeWitt Bank and Trust the new administrator.

After court is over, I find the one-room space in the courthouse that decades ago contained DeWitt's public library. I'd spent hours there in my childhood, chatting with Mrs. Miller, the librarian. She'd have selections waiting for me on her desk: the Bobbsey Twins, Andy Hardy, Nancy Drew. I came to love the smell of dust and history and benign neglect in the pages of those books. The space is used for a storeroom now; cardboard boxes rise almost to the ceiling.

Estrangement presents as a little death, like divorce. Estrangement from my sister means, among a host of other things, that I no longer hear her laugh. Through the years, Nancy's quick wit comprised a significant part of my well-being. In our adult lives, we'd managed to get together at least once a month, and when my daughter was fifteen, she, Nancy, and I drove through Maine, New Hampshire, and Vermont. (I was forever lost; Nancy had an uncanny sense of direction.) Years later, my sister and

I met occasionally in Kansas City to shop consignment-clothing stores. Nancy gravitated toward black outfits, simply cut—"the better," she'd declare, to "show the jewelry off." We'd scour Kansas City for antiques, marveling at each other's zany purchases.

THE FIRE OF DRIFT-WOOD

. . . .The long-lost ventures of the heart,
That send no answers back again.

—HENRY W. LONGFELLOW

Charles and I navigate old Highway 71, two-lane and treacherous, curling through the quietly spectacular Ozark Mountains of northwest Arkansas, on our way back to Kansas. By this time, April or May of 1996, the estate has limped along for almost two years, no resolution in sight. We've left the hills of Edgemont, the Delta towns of Stuttgart and DeWitt, the hustle of Little Rock. In the dimming light, I grade essay papers while Charles drives, but I can't concentrate on subject-verb agreement or dangling modifiers. I'm reliving the depositions, the courtroom, the attorneys' voices. As dusk takes the mountains, a bird call—high, remote, sweet—pierces the noise of the car. My sister is lost to me.

CHAPTER 7

Town

My earliest memories of DeWitt are its driveways. Mother maintained a milk-and-egg route in town; in the summer and on Saturdays, I'd go with her to make deliveries. She sold cream, milk, and hen's eggs with brown or white shells. The money from this enterprise she kept for her very own—my early introduction, in the 1940s, to women's lib. Some of Mother's customers lived in large houses with expansive driveways that seemed to me, as a child, as vast as airport runways. At each stop, Mother and the woman of the house would stand outside to chat. Simply for being there, for smiling and saying little, I was the object of much attention and undeserved praise.

The meticulous preparations for these trips to town began in Mother's kitchen. Every Saturday, it was teeming with the smell of warm milk, and in one corner would sit an oversized basket of eggs. Mother persuaded the cream from the milk with a separator, a clumsy apparatus she remained constantly at odds with, then bottled the milk and cream, wiping each bottle clean.

Bob Wright milked the cows and brought the milk to the kitchen. One of Dad's overworked, scantily paid farm workers, Bob was a bachelor, something of a loner, inexplicably loyal to my father and devoted to my mother. He had come to the farm to maintain the Fairbanks, succeeding Virgil Howe, another hired hand, who had relinquished the post after only one season. Mother fussed over Bob, seeing to it he had milk and eggs to take back to the pumping shed, where he had set up housekeeping.

My role in Mother's milk-and-egg business consisted of gathering eggs from the reluctant hens—hoping not to be pecked, dodging the droppings in the henhouse, forbearing the arrogant roosters. My father said foxes came in the night to the henhouse. I never witnessed one, but I often saw the broken eggshells in their wake.

After the bottles of milk and cream were labeled and deemed spotless, after the eggs had been washed and washed again, Mother and I would set off for town, scattering the thick dust of the road in which might be engraved the trail of a snake. Once we crossed the railroad track, we were almost to the highway. Roughly three miles lay between our house and the outskirts of DeWitt.

I delighted in those excursions. I would campaign to be dropped off at the courthouse, so I could visit the library, or at the house of a friend. But most of the time Mother insisted I go with her on her route, "to get to know these people." In this way I met the sisterhood of women who helped weave my childhood world—matrons, businesswomen, mothers of my friends, teachers who took an interest in my well-being. One of the retired teachers on Mother's route, Helen Davis, had taught my father in high school.

I came to know the driveways and back porches of Mother's customers, their faces and mannerisms and voices, as well as I knew the furniture in my room. DeWitt was, as in the *Vision of Piers Plowman,* my "fair field full of folk"; there I found "all manner of men, the mean and the rich / working and wandering, as the world asks." Among the fewer than three thousand souls living in DeWitt between 1940 and 1950 were shopkeepers, housewives, house painters, accountants, lumberjacks, bankers, drifters, lawyers, waitresses, carpenters, grocers, embalmers, preachers, hoboes, farmers, teachers, butchers, blacksmiths, salesmen, mechanics, grain brokers, deputies, dishwashers—young and old, ambitious and shiftless alike. Along Mother's route lived families—not all of them her customers—whose names indicated a variety of nationalities: Kirkendoff, Spratlin, Quertermous, Pike, Boone, Bullock, Vansandt, Kagebein, Woodiel, Capps, Leibrock, Aufderheide, Barr, Botts, Howe, Kidd, Essex, LaFargue, Pattillo, Fulton, Kirchoff, Chambers, Blackmon, Kittler, Gunnell, Kendall, Hageman, Sanders, Rousseau, Stephenson, Ferguson, Thigpen, Carnes—to name only a few.

Mother's customers seemed always happy to see her. Her products were fresh; at the time of delivery, the milk and eggs had scarcely left the cow and chickens. Although Mother hadn't grown up in DeWitt, she had come from a farming background and didn't "put on airs." In 1964, having stepped away from teaching home economics in the St. Charles and DeWitt high schools, Mother opened up her shop on the square. Until her death in 1985, her former customers and/or their daughters came in to gossip and sometimes to buy.

———

On these forays with Mother, I learned not only DeWitt's houses but also its businesses: Eula Bonner's Millinery, Merritt's Grocery, Schallhorn's Hardware, Shackelford's Grocery and Frozen Storage, Danner's Tuf-Nut Store, Lorick's Dry Goods, "Fibber" McGhie's sundries, and a five-and-dime with creaking hardwood floors named, as best I remember, the Broken Dollar. At the entrance, I could weigh myself on an ornately decorated scale for a penny.

Mrs. Rothenhofer's Café, which sat in one corner of the square, was the scene of my fifth or sixth birthday party. Mother coached me that I must thank every one in person for my gifts. If invited to a party, I was sternly instructed to thank the honoree and his or her mother for asking me. When Mother picked me up, she never failed to ask if I had done so. If I'd forgotten, she would proclaim, horrified, that I had been "rude," or even worse, "tacky," and would send me back to properly take my leave. Those birthday parties were the reinforcement of a Southern social code that begins in the cradle.

DeWitt's only movie theater offered its refuge at the end of a short alley, Little Broadway, which angled in front of Rothenhofer's. It went by various names, but in my day it was called the New Theatre. To most of us, however, it was known simply as "the Show," as in, "I'll meet you at the Show." Recently I ran across a program from the 1942 senior play at DeWitt High School. The New Theatre, an advertiser, announced Ginger Rogers and Roxie Hart as coming attractions.

Television wouldn't invade most DeWitt homes until the 1950s. We watched, instead, the yellow dial of the radio, matching voices to faces we imagined. Entertainment could also be found at the roller-skating rink with its fake-sounding, piped-in organ music. I vaguely remember a minstrel show, probably held as a fund-raiser for the all-white Lions or

Rotarians. In the summers, for a few weeks, a carnival set up shop on the outskirts of DeWitt, on fairgrounds known as Camp Doughboy. Sometimes a third-rate circus would lumber into town, but for the most part, we depended upon the movies to liberate us from boredom.

It was at "the Show" that I saw the movie *Ghost of Frankenstein*. I was probably seven or eight. I came home skewered with fright. That fear was exacerbated when I went to bed. In the shadows caused by a stingy night-light, I saw something small, ethereal and yet skeletal, buzz across the ceiling. It was probably a wasp tangled in a spiderweb, but it sent me into panic. After Mother had calmed me, she decreed, "That's the last Frankenstein movie you'll be going to, young lady, I can tell you that."

I was not quite six when the United States entered World War II, in 1941. Following the main feature at the theater, Pathé News and R.K.O. brought us carefully edited news of the war in black and white, narrated in a monotonous tone reminiscent of *National Geographic*. In these propaganda pieces, our boys and allies were always doing well in Europe or the Philippines or the South Pacific.

———

DeWitt lies, according to one observer writing anonymously in the DeWitt paper in 1925, "buried at the southern end of the matchless Grand Prairie." The observer is writing in praise of "the capital city of one of the oldest counties in Arkansas, a county that dates its existence six years beyond the date of the organization of the Arkansaw Territory." Situated in a landscape of river bottoms, lakes, swamps, and sluggish bayous, DeWitt was, and is, host to thousands of hunters every hunting season. The land was wild, as were the men who inhabited it. The intrepid hunter and marksman Davy Crockett, passing through central Arkansas in 1835, is reported to have vowed, "If I could rest anywhere, it would be Arkansas, where the men are of the real half-horse, half-alligator breed such as grow nowhere else on the face of the universal earth."

According to C. F. Scott, editor-owner of the DeWitt paper, my hometown was named for New York's governor DeWitt Clinton, whose name was drawn out of a hat. It was founded in 1853 and designated the Arkansas County seat when, as Scott observes, "Arkansas Post's importance dwindled." DeWitt pulled in trade from neighboring Gillett, St. Charles, Almyra, Casscoe, Ethel, Lodge Corner, Crocketts Bluff (named for a grandson of Davy Crockett), Van, and Brewer Bottoms. In my childhood, its business district marched snaggle-toothed around the courthouse square. Traffic proceeded only one way around the square, but on Saturday nights the more daring of DeWitt's young men would drive it in reverse. They also drove with their windows up in the summer, hoping to fool the girls into thinking they had air-conditioned cars.

DeWitt's courthouses present a colorful history. The present-day structure, a somber fixture of my childhood and the centerpiece of the town square, was completed in 1932. A three-story building of yellow brick, it's the last of a procession—from early log buildings, to a square, brick building, to a compelling baroque structure built in 1893. This nineteenth-century structure eventually proved faulty and had to be demolished, but the metal statue that reigned as its capital adornment still exists, the subject of much speculation and mystery. According to the late Garner Allen, long-time member of the Grand Prairie Historical Society, the statue is thought to be of the Greek goddess Astraea, with a spear in one hand and the scales of justice in the other. Pockmarked with bullet holes from vandals circling the square on horseback, the statue abided for a time in Arkansas Post Lake as "Lady of the Lake." It's supposedly in private hands now, awaiting restoration. The clock from the destroyed courthouse lives on in the exterior of its predecessor. Fully restored, the clock has all-brass works and keeps reliable time.

As a child, I was fascinated and perplexed by the Art Deco floral-and-zigzag motifs in concrete panels framing the courthouse entrances. I remember that its hallways smelled of marble, brass, sweat, and spit. The large trees now shading the courthouse were saplings in my childhood; in summers the courthouse stood naked, vandalized by the sun.

———

Home to a distinctive courthouse, DeWitt also was home to an equally notable drugstore. Among the several drugstores in the community as I was growing up, Snarr's Drugs ("In Business for Your Health") was, for me, the most memorable. The sound of the name—prickly, slightly ominous—lodged in my imagination. Located on the square, Snarr's, for all the homeliness of its name, was an oasis. Its mosaic-tiled floors, dark wood, and shadowy corners provided a reprieve from summer's witless heat. Since the majority of DeWitt's houses and businesses weren't air-conditioned until the mid-1950s, when I was in my teens, I spent most of my childhood looking for shade. Even now I measure a property's worth by the number of shade trees it offers.

One of the town's general practitioners, Dr. R. H. Whitehead, had his office in the back of Snarr's. He was one of a trio of DeWitt's somber-faced doctors whom I remember. Dr. Homer Dickens, a friend of my dad, occasionally had our family over for supper, and I was impressed that he could read documents written in Greek. Dr. C. W. Rasco, the father of one of my classmates, came from an old DeWitt family; his father had been a medical doctor before him—a "good, old-time country doctor." These doctors made house calls, but I remember Mother rushing me to Dr. Rasco's office one Saturday afternoon when I was five. I'd been running from a young woman Mother employed—and whom I detested—when I collided with a hasp lock on the wash-shed door, slicing my forehead. The doctor's office was bright and sparse, its white enamel cabinets full of sinister instruments. I froze when he reached into one of the cabinets, sure I would not leave the office alive. I survived, and Dr. Rasco gave me a red penny sucker for being "so good" while he stitched the gash.

In the company of my mother, I met the women of the town. In the company of my father, I met the men. "Frenchy" Trichell, the small-repairs shop owner, was one of my dad's favorites. "Buster" Hobbs, who worked at A. R. Thorell's International Harvester dealership, was one of mine. When I came into the door of Thorell's with Daddy, Buster would kid me about my pigtails. Then he would lift me onto the newest red tractor in the showroom; it gave off the self-important, slick smell of new paint and steel.

Since the early 1900s, the growing of rice had been DeWitt's, and indeed Arkansas County's, largest industry. It drove the town's economy. The International Harvester dealership was one of numerous suppliers selling tractors, combines, plows, discs, and other equipment to DeWitt's farmers. My father frequented them all: Hiram Johnson's Case dealership, L. A. Black's John Deere agency, and the dealers for Allis-Chalmers, Massey-Harris, and Minneapolis-Moline. The huge machines seemed aloof, surrounded by stillness.

DeWitt supported more than one welding shop, but Daddy gave most of his business to Bateman's, located in a barn-red ramshackle building slanted beside a small, isolated scope of trees. It smelled always of electricity and grease.

Bumping around town in Dad's pickup, traveling streets with solid American names such as Jefferson, Maxwell, Adams, Monroe, Halliburton, Union, Washington, and Cross, we visited the Rice Belt Produce and Feed Company with its sweetish odors of meal and grain; the First National Bank with its high ceilings, hard-edged marble, and ambience of pomp; the Cormier Rice Mill; Chaney Motor Company; Chaney Lumber Company; and the post office, which smelled of new paper and glue. I was proud to walk into those businesses beside my father, entering a man's world.

That world was dominated by L. A. ("Cap'n") Black, one of DeWitt's wealthiest and most influential men. His power stemmed from his vast holdings of Arkansas County farmland, obtained in great part by paying delinquent back taxes on farms during the Depression. Some townspeople, including my father, admired and respected him; others reviled him. One of the tantamount pieces of DeWitt gossip occurred after Mr. Black's death in the mid-1940s. His three daughters, in line for a sizeable fortune in land and other assets, entered into a dispute over their inheritance that lasted for decades and resulted in estrangement between two of the sisters. Ironically, toward the end of Daddy's life, Nancy and I vowed that we would never allow such a thing to happen to us.

My grandfather Garot, a friend of Mr. Black, had himself held a position of influence and respect in DeWitt as one of its pioneer rice farmers. A man of generosity and contagious good spirit, known to all as "Uncle Joe," he had numerous friends in town. After retiring to Hot Springs, he and Grandmother came back to DeWitt often, staying with us in the upstairs guest room. I would beg to ride with Granddad when he paid calls in DeWitt. His Chevrolet (replaced by the all-desirable

Buick in the late 1940s) was dusty inside and out, its seats upholstered in a frizzy, unfriendly fabric, its gray headliner punctuated by a domed, useless interior light. I thought it a wondrous vehicle.

Although I can't remember who lived there, I could drive now to the house where, on one of those outings with Granddad, I fell into a fish pond. I was no more than five or six. I'd been standing in a yard with my grandfather and his friends; we were about to leave, but the goodbyes were long and convoluted, as they tend to be in the South. I grew bored and backed away. Suddenly I was over my head in water. "Jo!" I heard my grandfather shout. "Omigod! Jo!" I heard voices rising, someone shouting, "She's in the pond! She's in the water! Somebody get her!" Then I heard nothing. I saw light squiggling over my head and felt my grandfather's hand around my wrist, seizing it so hard it hurt, pulling me out of the water. I don't remember being afraid. "I'd like to have stayed there," I told Grandfather—after I'd been duly fussed over, put in dry clothes ten times too big, and bundled into the car for the ride home. "It was nice," I said. "It was so warm."

Mother was aghast at the sight of me. Her drowning phobia aroused, she scarcely spoke to my grandfather the rest of his visit.

I remember the lined and pleasant faces of the couple who owned the fish pond. They and other men and women of DeWitt became my extended family, a presence I simply received like day and night, like breathing. It seems to me that DeWitt rested on the fertile Arkansas Delta like a benevolent stain, a circle in the ground that its founders and rice-farming pioneers such as my grandfather had drawn—a fortress secure against an outside world I had yet to discover. Within that circle lived men and women devoted to routine, seemingly content in lives given to church, trade, family, local politics, potluck dinners, and—unless they were Baptist—occasional card games.

We, of course, were Methodist and therefore not under such constraints. Methodist girls could wear shorts if they wanted and could even go dancing. My family had a designated pew in the First United Methodist church, the church that so defined my father, the institution to which Granddad Garot donated stained-glass windows and a chancel rail, the place where I would meet Charles and where we would marry.

It pleased me whenever the sun angled through those windows configured with ribbons, Jesus, lambs, and angels, their blue-and-red primary colors heightened. Indeed, sunlight transformed each window into a Coat of Many Colors, streaming across the faces of the congregation. Dad, tall and straight in his dark suit, passed the collection plate every Sunday, pausing solemnly at each pew. He considered this task more a privilege than a duty. When I was very small, I carried every week to church my contribution, usually a nickel, knotted in one corner of a crisp white handkerchief.

It was in this church that I experienced my first intense crush. In 1949, when I was fourteen, the church hired a youth director for the summer. Probably just out of college, the new director had blond hair, a deep tan, and a Van Johnson smile. More important, he was a stranger and an Older Man. I'd had wispy encounters with the opposite sex before—a brush of a kiss in first grade, a crush on a boy who rode my school bus, a fascination with a football player who could play "Flight of the Bumble Bee" on the piano—but my feelings for the director were different. Here attraction was coupled with religious fervor. When he looked my way one evening in church and smiled, I decided I would run away with him and witness for the Lord—never mind that I hadn't yet been asked by either party. Fortunately my parents talked me down from that cloud. By fall the youth director had left DeWitt, and I'd begun dating Charles.

Dad taught the Methodist church men's Sunday-school class, and I played the piano for them. I played abominably, fumbling the notes as if wearing welder's gloves, but the men trudged valiantly on, off-key. Together we trounced Methodism's staunchest hymns: "Onward, Christian Soldiers," "Blessed Assurance," "Bringing in the Sheaves," and "The Old Rugged Cross," Daddy's favorite.

After church my folks and I sometimes ate dinner in DeWitt's main hotel, located just off the square. In DeWitt and other farming communities, the noon meal was designated as "dinner" and the evening meal as "supper." The word "lunch" was almost never used, implying food too fancy and too light to stick to your ribs. The hotel's specialty was chicken and dumplings and overcooked roast beef with ho-hum mashed potatoes and brown gravy. The dining room was splendid with starched white tablecloths. It was also the setting for the Rotary Club and the Lions Club, and one fall Dad and I took a Dale Carnegie course there.

SMALL TOWN AT DUSK

Night takes the sidewalks first
and then the marigolds and the sprinklers,
the children's skates.
Nothing argues with the ambling dogs
except the tree frogs and the occasional slamming
of a screen door.

Two of my closest childhood friends in DeWitt were Meredith Miller
and Gay Hudspeth. Meredith's mother, the librarian, was a colleague of
my mother in the Women's Study Club. Mr. Miller was an accountant
for one of the local rice mills. Theirs was an all-American family in an
all-American two-story white house with shutters, an ample front yard,
and a long, sloping backyard peopled with evergreens.

When I stayed overnight with Meredith, her father made us milk-
shakes before bed. We would all sit at the kitchen table talking as Mrs.
Miller rolled Meredith's long blond hair on rags, making sausage curls.
Books lounged everywhere. Sometimes Meredith and I would each take
one and, the family cat sprawled at our feet, fall asleep reading in bed.

Until I was fifteen and she moved away, Gay Hudspeth and I played
together almost every time Mother went to town. Gay lived with her
grandmother Morrow ("Granny") and her aunt Frances in a slightly shabby
house with sloping floors and one tiny bathroom. The house sat angled
across from the Methodist church. Gay and I often played hopscotch on
the church's uneven sidewalk, watched over by a row of sycamores.

When I was about fifteen, Mother insisted I take voice lessons from
Gay's aunt Frances. It was rumored Frances had lost her fiancé in the war,
although no one in that house ever spoke of it. I was immensely undertal-

ented in the singing department, but Miss Frances persevered. Recently I heard an old recording of Mario Lanza singing "Be My Love," and Miss Frances's upright piano, the sheet music, and Frances herself—tall, slim, with shoulder-length, curly brown hair—rose before me. I was back in that sweet, disheveled house that smelled of clabbered milk, singing as Frances played "O Promise Me" or anything by Sigmund Romberg, my mind full of romantic visions, my voice improving not a mite.

Granny—short, round, bustling, her gray hair pulled into an untidy bun, her felt house slippers split at the sides to accommodate her bunions—ruled the house. She was never without her full-length apron, stained and aromatic from constant attendance at the cookstove. I adored Granny, and I think she viewed me almost as another granddaughter.

Granny's other daughter, Gay's mother, was in a sanitarium in Booneville, a victim of tuberculosis. I never met her, for her visits home were infrequent, but her photos were throughout the house. She was pretty, with an oval face and huge, dark eyes. No one ever spoke of Gay's father. This was a household full of secrets, tinged by sadness despite its laughter, run entirely by women.

Whenever Gay and I tired of playing records (78s) from Frances's sizable collection or grew bored with brushing Rusty, Gay's cocker spaniel, we would head down the rickety back stairs, past the chinaberry tree, to the drainage ditch that ran along the east side of Granny's yard. The ditch held greasy water of questionable origin, and Mother scolded me endlessly about playing near it. Polio was the rampant, overriding fear of my generation, at its peak in the mid-1940s through the early 1950s and thought to be acquired from unsanitary water. There were one or two cases in town. Gay and I played at the ditch anyway, careful never to touch the water, grateful for the tall oaks and willows along its banks that cut the sun to shreds and shadows. One lawn's length away was the street. We were oblivious to the traffic, lost in the jungle, comparing boyfriends and hairstyles and makeup.

The summer before Gay turned fifteen, her mother died. Frances quit giving voice lessons. The once lively house was subdued, like light through imperfect window glass. By the time school opened, Granny had spirited her household away to St. Charles, Missouri. In Mother's attic, I found correspondence from Gay after she had moved, full of enthusiasm for her new life and the fun she was having.

In a letter postmarked August 24, 1951, when we are both about sixteen, Gay asks how I'm wearing my hair now, what my plans are for college, and says she's "still collecting records. . . . My favorite is still Harry James." "Do you have TV yet?" she inquires. "I just love it but it really interferes with homework." She relates that she "went to a ball game today and saw the Browns play the Boston Red Sox. I got to see Ted Williams real close & is he cute! (but he has a horrible temper. He struck out once & got so mad he broke the bat on the ground)."

When I re-read the letter, nearly fifty years after it was written, I remembered my feelings of loss and desertion when Gay left DeWitt. If she wrote of anything good that happened in her new life, I refused to believe a word. After a stay in Missouri, Granny and company moved to someplace in Texas, and Gay and I lost touch.

———

There were other childhood friends, of course—friends with bag swings in their backyards, exotic parents who played golf, capricious cats and ugly but lovable dogs and pesky younger brothers. Some of my friends' older sisters taught us how to ballroom dance and jitterbug; I thought these young women glamorous and worldly beyond belief. One, Jo Ann Rodgers, often hosted her younger sister's bunking parties in her farmhouse near DeWitt. Boys—the ones who drove the square in reverse—would come by after midnight, honking their horns and shining their cars' headlights into the windows. Before long, the head of the house, Johnny Rodgers—furious and in his pajamas—would plant himself in the driveway, shake his fists, and shout, "Bygod, so help me, I'm calling every last one of your fathers."

Another close friend, Shirley Gillcoatt, lived on a farm west of DeWitt, near the One-Horse Store, a relic from the days of the retailing staple, the general store. Situated at a dirt crossroads, the store carried everything from overalls to oatmeal. It had survived the changing habits of consumers, a stalwart anachronism. On hot days Shirley and I would bicycle down to the One-Horse, scoop two bottled Cokes from the metal lift-top cooler, and wander barefoot around the store. Its wood floors were warm and satiny, smoothed by generations of amblers.

All my girlfriends liked to come to the farm on summer days to swim in the weir (containment) pond. Water to irrigate the rice was pumped from deep in the ground, collected in the pond, and funneled along irrigation ditches, finally reaching the growing rice. The water smelled like a mix of raw oysters and prehistoric mud and, at fifty-eight to sixty degrees, was cold enough to send lightning through our brains. Plunging into that water, coming out into the volcanic heat, we had the ultimate sauna experience, though we'd never heard of such a thing.

1942

My father's harmonica came off the mantel every night.
He played it while my mother sang
until they went to bed.
The last songs were always
"Working on the Railroad," "O Susanna,"
and "Sam," a song my mother invented.
Whenever the paper said
someone in our town was killed
or missing in action,
my father wouldn't take the harmonica down
even if
it was no one we knew.

When World War II ended in 1945, Mother showed me the headlines in the *Arkansas Gazette,* bigger and blacker than any I had ever seen, nearly consuming the front page. I was scarcely aware of what it all meant.

The four years of U.S. involvement in the war, however, had affected me in profound ways. I knew that some of the windows of DeWitt held blue stars, meaning a member of the household was in the service. Some held gold stars: the soldier wouldn't be coming back.

World War II helped shape my life: the songs—some wryly playful ("Praise the Lord, and Pass the Ammunition"), some heartbreaking ("I'll Be Seeing You"); the glimpses of chaos and loss; the changes in culture and fashion; the romance. Even at a young age, I sensed that in a wartime world everything is risked and anything is possible—at least, that's the way it was in the movies. Then there was the seductive aura of the uniform. Even my corpulent uncle Coy looked dashing in army khakis.

For many young women older than I, the war was truly the defining moment in their lives. Near Stuttgart (named for Germany's Stuttgart by German Lutherans in 1889 but pronounced in Arkansas with a short *u*), the army built an airport in 1942 to train glider pilots. Many girls in the region fell in love with pilots stationed there, some of whom came back to Arkansas after the war, married their wartime sweethearts, and became agri pilots, better known as cropdusters.

Dropping close to ground to deliver herbicide or fertilizer over a rice field, pulling almost straight up to clear trees, pickups, power lines, or cows, these pilots sometimes found themselves in as much danger as they'd known in combat. Occasionally, I flagged for my father, holding a marker at the ends of rows to orient the pilot. I'd be terrified when a plane pulled straight up from the ground and over my head, missing me by what seemed to be mere inches. Still, I was spellbound by the pilot's spectacular maneuvers. Every farmer dreaded that a pilot would snag a tree limb or power line and crash on his farm, in flames.

———

Over my mother's vehement protests, Dad learned to fly, taking instruction from a crop duster at Smith and Jones Flying Service, located near our farm. Sometimes Dad would take me with him to the airstrip when he took his lessons. I caught the bug. While I was at Stephens, I, too, learned to fly, going out to the field at seven A.M., before classes. Mother was much opposed to this, but Dad encouraged me. Despite a memorable ground loop caused by a crosswind, I eventually soloed in a Piper Cub.

———

Much of the terminology of World War II I didn't understand—terms such as "fox hole," "black market," "pill box," "war bonds." Sometime during the war, the movie star Dick Powell (supposedly born in Mountain View) came to DeWitt. I remember him on the stage of the movie theater, debonair in a pin-striped suit. I surmise now that he was there to sell bonds.

Rationing, of course, I did understand. Without gas, we wouldn't be going into town. "Is this trip really necessary?" was pasted on the windshield of our Chevrolet. To show his patriotism, Grandfather Garot, ever the artist, fashioned a metal V (for Victory), studded it with red-and-blue reflector buttons, and attached it to the bumper of his car. Mother kept close tabs on her ration books, complaining about the scarcity of sugar and nylons. To give the illusion of wearing stockings, the more daring of the girls in DeWitt High painted black "seams" down the backs of their legs.

Toward the end of the conflict, we lived in the ominous shadow of the draft. At the onset of the war, Dad, being a farmer, married, and with a child, was safe from conscription. Farmers were considered essential on the home front, and the government, early on, took only young, single men. But as the fighting wore on, as more and more American men were lost, the draft was widened to include men who'd heretofore been exempt, even those who, like my father, were in their thirties.

"What do you think, Leon?" Mother would sometimes ask after supper, as she and Daddy sat listening to the radio, thinking I was out of earshot. "Do you think you'll have to go? They're saying . . ." "I don't know, Ruth. How should I know?" my father would snap, getting up to change the station. I would leave my post at the top of the stairs and plunge into bed, my world darkening. The war ended, however, without Dad being called up.

My father's exempt status as a farmer caused some hard feelings in DeWitt. I remember a raffle in 1942 or 1943—I was seven or eight—that was held on the courthouse grounds. My father, who swore he "never won anything," won the prize of several hundred dollars. Most people applauded, but I heard someone mutter, "That money ought to go to somebody who needs it, not to some draft dodger." I asked Mother what "draft dodger" meant. Her eyes narrowing, she hissed, "We're leaving. Get in the car." I didn't press for an answer.

During those years of the war, Daddy kept to his task, planting and harvesting, watering the rice, checking the levees in high-topped rubber boots, stepping around cottonmouths. The crops came; the crops went. Dad left the house at dawn, returning at dark—during harvest, as late as nine or ten P.M.—sweaty and cross, dirt and rice dust framing his mouth and eyes.

World War II finally ended. DeWitt took a deep breath, counted its dead, and welcomed back its wounded. Our cousin Victor came back from France to farm, living in the house of his mother. (For a brief time, he operated a popcorn stand in front of the bank building that would house Gallery G.) My uncle Coy shed his uniform and tried, unsuccessfully, to find some purpose in his life, coming briefly to farm with my dad, living in a trailer beside the railroad tracks.

It strikes me as odd now that I never heard my parents—well educated, subscribers to the local and state papers, informed by the nightly radio news—discuss Pearl Harbor, Auschwitz, Bataan, the Normandy invasion, or Hiroshima. While these events changed the world forever, I was roller skating on the front walk and learning to ride my bike. I rode the yellow school bus home every day to listen to my favorite soap operas—*Stella Dallas* and *The Guiding Light,* sponsored by Lux, Rinso (Rinso-Bright!), and Ipana toothpaste.

It was hard to escape the psychological fallout of the atomic bomb, however. It eclipsed polio as the Gila monster of our world. Ads for bomb shelters appeared everywhere. When I was fourteen or fifteen and a dutiful member of 4-H, I traveled to Fayetteville in July for the state convention, stayed at the university's historic Carnall Hall in a stifling second-story room, and delivered a speech on the effects of the atom bomb on my generation. I won a blue ribbon.

———

As if to offset the gloom of the bomb, the 1940s marked a turn in women's fashions. The somewhat shapeless dresses of the thirties were ousted by ones accenting the body. I was dimly aware of this. Drawn to fashion even at a young age, I studied the mannequins in the windows of Lorick's Dry Goods and Bonner's Millinery every time we went to town. The real learning laboratory, however, was DeWitt high school.

I remember older girls at DeWitt high wearing suits with padded shoulders, sharply accented waists, and peplums. I envied their high heels, sling-backed and open-toed. I remember snoods for the hair (often called "fascinators" for some inexplicable reason) and "rats," soft, long rolls around which the hair would be swept up and wrapped. The "Eisenhower" jacket, named for General Eisenhower's World War II field jacket, swept the fashion world. Cropped at the waist and slightly bloused, it became a staple in my closet by the time I was fifteen, when I became truly fashion obsessed. The 1950s ushered in a new look: the slim skirts of the 1940s gave way to circle skirts, worn over numerous crinoline petticoats.

When I entered Stephens in 1953—the year DeWitt turned one hundred—the item I favored most in my wardrobe was a black *matelassé* silk, full-skirted dress with an elasticized cinch belt. With it I wore a black felt cartwheel hat. The 1940s had been an era of saucy, inventive hats, and the custom of wearing them held until the 1960s. Stephens, being a school for women, promoted afternoon teas, and students were expected to dress for them in cocktail dresses, hats, and gloves. The star in my hat wardrobe was the cartwheel, purchased at Rosenthal's dress shop in Stuttgart. It reminded me of the creations Scarlett wore, pre–Civil War, in *Gone with the Wind*.

Mother supported my interest in fashion, but when it came to my wearing lipstick, she balked. I was probably fourteen when I discovered Elizabeth Arden lipstick—"Blush Pink," the most mesmerizing color I had ever seen—on Mother's cosmetic shelf. I applied it, entering the grown-up world—but briefly—and incurring Mother's wrath.

———

Being fifteen and one of the last girls in my crowd to wear color on my lips, I resorted countless times to the teenager's tiresome plea, "But *everybody's* doing it!" Many battles ensued. I hounded Mother for months; finally, in one of the zenith moments of my adolescence, Mother said I could wear lipstick—sparingly—on Sundays. I can still feel the empowerment of that small, silvery case in my pocket.

I had learned at an early age that "looking good"—by whatever shifting standards that was measured—didn't come easily. By the time I was five, I was subjected to the rigors of the permanent wave, in La Cotts (pronounced "La Cutts") Beauty Shop, a block or two, as I remember, off DeWitt's square. Shirley Temple was the child star of the period, and

Mother was determined I would have Shirley Temple curls. My hair—thin, fine, and pencil straight—was placed, clump by listless clump, in wave clamps dangling from electric wires. The wires attached to a hood shaped like an inverted bowl; the whole affair hung from the ceiling like a medieval tool of torture. (This was before the Toni—chemistry's miracle home permanent that eliminated the need for such contraptions.) The smell as chemicals and heat seared my hair was worse than that of mule urine, and the curls were tight and frizzy. Mother was delighted, but I hated the bramble patch that was now my hair.

I adored, however, the clothes Mother bought me at "Miss Bonner's." For my first piano recital, when I was six, Mother and Ms. Bonner outfitted me in a brown taffeta dress with trapunto stitching on the bodice and an ecru-lace Peter Pan collar. The taffeta rustled when I walked. For all its style and rustling, though, the dress couldn't alleviate the panic of being on stage and forgetting three-fourths of "Clair de Lune." My piano teacher, Mrs. Ila Hemingway, had, at the beginning of the year, high hopes for my musical career. Dutifully, I went for weekly lessons in her drafty studio behind the stage of the high school auditorium. For "excellent progress," she awarded me a hand-painted music box that played "La Traviata." After the recital, Mrs. Hemingway threatened to take the award back, vowing she'd made a mistake.

I had experienced panic before that recital, of course, notably in Ms. Bird Wright's kindergarten. When Mother was late to pick me up—which was often—I was sure I'd been abandoned. I would cry nonstop until I saw Mother's car, much to the chagrin of "Miss Bird," a tall, dear, cheerful woman who did her best to console me.

In 1941, I entered first grade. I was a talker, chattering on with my friends even after Miss Jessie Lee Wimberly, young and inexperienced, had called for class to begin. Punishment for such an offense was to be put in a corner of the classroom on a high stool with one's back to the class. I saw the corner the first day and on countless days ensuing. I cried each time, crushed at the indignity.

———

A more profound event, however, befell me in the second grade. Although I made good grades and spelling was my strong suit, I looked across the aisle one morning at a friend's paper during a spelling test. Of course I was spotted by the teacher, the wintry Mrs. Zelma Miles. She said nothing to me until it was time for recess, then commanded, "Keep your seat." Shame flogged me as my classmates filed past, each one taking a full century. *Cheat* was branded on my forehead. When the last student was out the door, Mrs. Miles told me calmly that she would say "nothing now" but would "most definitely" report this to my mother. Fortunately or unfortunately, depending on one's viewpoint, the teachers and parents of DeWitt had a strong working relationship.

The lecture at home was worse than being dipped in flaming oil. Then guilt set in. I began to understand the meaning of God's wrath: I would die within the week and go to Hell for my sin. For months I silently beseeched God for a long life—in my nightly prayers, at recess, running errands with my mother, brushing my teeth—promising over and over: "Lord, if you'll just let me live until I'm forty and not send me to Hell, I will never cheat in school again."

I excelled in school, eventually becoming salutatorian of my graduating class, but I did poorly in sports and in all things calling for coordination. In the ninth grade I joined the band, adopting the clarinet simply because my folks deemed it one of the less expensive instruments to rent. One week after I joined, the Dewitt High School band marched in the Cotton Carnival in Memphis. I was nearly immobilized with fear that I would wobble out of line or out of step. I held the clarinet to my mouth, fingered some keys, but ventured not a sound. Subsequent months of practice in the colorless band room and on the early-morning football field didn't help; I never mastered the art of marching and playing at the same time.

There were compensations for my misery in the band. On one band trip to Hot Springs, we stayed in a derelict hotel that, somebody said, doubled as a whorehouse. This gave us something to withhold from our mothers and toss casually into conversation, for weeks.

In my carefree days before joining the band, I'd attended DeWitt's high school football games for fun, going there with my girlfriends, taking in the snap of fall weather, the frisson of excitement upon seeing our team in uniforms and helmets—though I understood nothing about football except touchdowns.

Under the spectators' bleachers lived an edgy world having little to do with the offices of the DHS playing field. Beneath the weathered planks lay liberty for all—quick kisses, smokes, fistfights, unbridled cussing—a universe, as if by mutual consent, off-limits to adults. The klieg lights that turned the grass of the field a surreal yellow lost momentum here, as diffused and fragmented as my friends and I, who were no longer children and not yet teens.

———

Although I was never to be proficient as a band member or in sports, I was ardent about language and writing. I was fortunate to have teachers who devoured literature and who discussed with me the essays I wrote, as well as those in our sage-green textbook of the best American literature. Together, we employed what would later come to be called critical thinking.

I became an editor of the school newspaper, the *DeWitt Hi-Times*, learned basic Latin, and achieved a respectable words-per-minute score in typing. All my high school teachers—Ethyl Oates Miller, Anna Robinson, June Fox, Martha Graves—encouraged my interest in creative writing, although the term hadn't yet been invented.

In those days Lion Oil Corporation sponsored an essay contest for high school seniors in Arkansas, Tennessee, and Mississippi, the prize being a scholarship to the college of one's choice. I was the winner from my school, much to the joy of my parents. I wrote on the assigned topic, the responsibility of every American citizen to help improve education. The judges must have relished being bored.

———

THE SUIT

> Awake, asleep,
> the woman dreams a suit to its perfection.
> . . . .
> . . . [T]he woman and the suit
> wait for each other.

It burns to sit upon her shoulders,
to button itself around her ribs.

———————————

Mother thought it imperative that young girls learn dressmaking skills.
The summer I was fourteen, she apprenticed me to a farm family outside
of DeWitt—the Glenn Alter family—who lived in an imposing two-
story house with tall trees in the yard. The house and the trees gave off
an aura of permanence, as if they'd been there since God created light.
I stayed weeks at a time with the Alters, learning more than sewing.
Cooking was this family's specialty. Daily, at noon, the three generations
of women in that house served up a meal for family and farmhands that
was the equivalent of Thanksgiving dinner. The daughter of the family,
Katie, was older than I, an accomplished seamstress who helped me sew
my first garment, a pull-over apron, and showed me how to scallop the
neckline of a linen blouse.

My favorite dressmaking project from that summer was a two-piece
outfit that I modified. Simplicity, a time-honored company and a household word, provided the pattern for a dirndl skirt and cap-sleeved blouse.
Suggested fabric was chambray or polished cotton. I thought, however,
that the ensemble would be stunning done up in pillow ticking. With
Katie's help, I stitched the garment in a blue-and-white cotton ticking, the
thickness of pre-tanned leather. At the sleeves, boat neck, and lower half
of the bodice, I stitched rows of red-ball fringe—an inspired use, I thought,
for curtain trim. I looked like a mattress with a waist, but I wore the outfit
everywhere. Looking back, I'm impressed with the patience of Katie, probably four years my senior, who helped me cut fabric to a pattern, pin and
baste, and operate a sewing machine without stitching a finger.

———————————

Undertaken as a 4-H project when I was about fifteen, tailoring a winter
suit posed a daunting challenge. For guidance, Mother enlisted the help
of a cousin, Gertrude Bell, who had a reputation for expert tailoring. The
project involved a wool-tweed fabric, set-in sleeves (a lesson in endurance),

bound buttonholes, and flat-fell seams. The suit, put together in weeks of after-school afternoons and Saturdays, must have worn my cousin out but won for me a 4-H award, my mother's approval, and a nod from DeWitt's premier dressmaker, Mrs. F. E. Mouton.

Mrs. F.E.—I never heard her called by any other name—was Grandfather Garot's sister, one of the clan who had come to DeWitt from Belgium. She was prematurely gray, and her skin seemed to match her hair. Short, dignified, not one to give away smiles, she made wondrous garments for Mother and me and later for my sister. Many of her creations went with me to college. I was in awe that my cousin could sketch a garment on the back of an envelope and take it to completion without using a store-bought pattern.

Mother decided Mrs. F.E. should have the last word on the suit; if it met with her approval, I could show it at the upcoming regional 4-H fashion event. The Moutons lived one block east of Maxie's Ice Cream Parlor, just off the square, next to a livestock-auction barn. We walked onto their nickel-sized front porch and knocked on the screen door; there wasn't a doorbell. "Come in," a voice called. "The door's open."

We were met with the odors of new fabric, onions, and vegetable soup. In the bedroom, at her treadle Singer, the town's best dressmaker held court. An oversized wrought-iron bed, painted ivory, dominated the room. Over it hung the figure of Christ on the cross and a framed print of Franklin Delano Roosevelt.

Mother explained the purpose of our visit. My cousin looked up from the Singer as I offered her the suit, presenting it as if it were some sacred vestment. It was a skirted suit, of course. No one in DeWitt wore pantsuits in the 1950s; those were for the likes of Katherine Hepburn and Greta Garbo.

"So," Mrs. F.E. said, her face implacable. "Let's take a look." My palms began to sweat. I was an acolyte in the dressmaking temple, and if I had not taken the craft seriously, I was about to be found out. In the silence, I could hear Mrs. F.E's husband, Mr. F.E., scuttling down the hall. With three or four straight pins pursed in her mouth, the veteran dressmaker turned the suit jacket inside out, unstitched a portion of the lining, and checked the seams. No one spoke. She checked the skirt. Mr. F.E. opened and shut a kitchen drawer. A car passed by, a sound like beginning rain. Finally, Mrs. F.E. removed the pins from her mouth. "Good," she pronounced, half frowning at me and nodding to Mother, stitching the linings of the jacket and skirt back with her nearly invisible blind stitch. I looked at Mother, who was beaming. The suit and I had passed.

At the time of the tailored-suit flurry, Nancy was four. I don't recall that she ever learned to sew; by the time of her coming of age in the 1960s, the world had changed. Women's lib, the hippies, the steady entry of women into the workforce had knocked the skills of cooking, tailoring, and dressing chickens off their pedestals. As I was perfecting homemaking and parenting, Nancy was at Dad's side, learning about ledgers and spreadsheets and hiring and firing personnel. She managed an apartment house Dad owned; later, she opened a day school—both in Little Rock, far from the relatively placid worlds of Stuttgart and DeWitt.

Perhaps my sister envied my accomplishments—average as they were—or perhaps she looked down on them. However she viewed them, a gap in our worlds and our cultural values had occurred, a gap that would be magnified in almost every way as Nancy and I sought jointly to manage Dad's estate.

———

Not far from the auction barn and Mrs. F.E.'s house sat Colored Town, officially a part of the city of DeWitt but unofficially another country, exotic and forbidden. It was understood that no white girl was to drive through its streets alone. Whites drove through on the way to St. Charles, about fifteen miles away; the men might stop briefly to solicit hired help. Of course, some white men visited Colored Town for sex, but nobody mentioned this.

Until I was married and in my late twenties, I knew no African Americans by name except Mary, who worked as my cousin Mollie's washwoman, and Beulah. Nor, for that matter, did I know anyone Jewish, except for the Stuttgart Rosenthals, until I went to college. Mother picked Beulah up one day a week, bringing her home always before sundown; it was considered improper for a white woman to be on that side of town after dark.

In DeWitt's businesses that I enjoyed freely, blacks deferred to whites, giving way in the aisles and at the cash registers, regardless of who got there first. Growing up, I don't remember ever looking into the eyes of a black person in the stores. As far as whites were concerned, African Americans had no names; they were there but invisible, as Ralph Ellison claimed. Blacks were not allowed to try on clothes, hats, or shoes in the stores, nor could they take them out on approval.

One of the boys in our all-white high school lived next door to a "colored" family. He was good-hearted, musically talented, and had no penchant for hunting or sports. It's hard to imagine which one of these egregious missteps ostracized him the most—the geography of his house or his disinterest in Southern boys' pastimes. After graduating from high school, he left DeWitt for Dallas and became an actor.

———

I was sixteen when I realized every American teenager's dream: driving. Daddy taught me on the back roads of the farm in his 1948 manual-shift pickup, his temper flaring as I grated through the gears. Eventually I was allowed to drive the pickup into DeWitt, but only for Sunday-evening church and Wednesday-evening Methodist Youth Fellowship. This was an extreme privilege in my father's eyes, but most of my friends not only had use of the family car but also were driving the twenty miles to Stuttgart. My father never expanded my driving privileges, but still I loved the solitude of driving the dirt roads, dust seeping in through the hand-cranked windows, a prairie sunset like a cape unfurling in slow motion, the sound of the tardy heater remembering what to do. The pickup had a chronic rattle, and springs sprouted through its vinyl bench seat. But I was driving. I was driving alone.

———

By most accounts, DeWitt has a history of violence: shootings in the movie theater on Saturday nights; a deputy killed by a bullet shot through the screen door of his house; mysterious bodies in the nearby rivers and bayous; and the case of the infamous Helen Spence, who, in the early 1930s, murdered her father's accused killer in the DeWitt courthouse as the killer was standing trial. By 1940, when I can first remember the community, it was relatively tame, a web of friendly voices, faces, and customs that spread over farm and town.

Like most small towns, DeWitt seemed to begin and end in a blur. As one was leaving its outskirts, it seemed to fray, its threads unraveling into woods and fields. On DeWitt's outlying farms were families with names almost as familiar as my own: Boyd, Fox, Muller, Miller, Thomas, Currie, Counce, Jessup, Eldridge, Simpson, Lumsden, Hargrove. There were a great many farmers; the rice and soybean industry was king in Arkansas County from the early 1900s until the 1980s. Indeed, DeWitt's neighbor Stuttgart was proclaimed the "Rice and Duck Capital of the World."

When I celebrated the end of World War II with my friends that summer afternoon in 1945, I looked down from the barn loft on what I perceived then to be my world: unending fields, the pumping shed, our house under its umbrella of pecans and elms. The house that my father's uncle Alex Lepine had built, rising stately across a neighboring field. Beyond and out of sight, the streets of DeWitt, my church, my school. Mattie Roy's boardinghouse. Colored Town. St. Charles and its reminders of Civil War battles. Arkansas Post, its romance and deep history, betrayed by a fickle river. Farms staked out by relatives who came to DeWitt at the turn of the twentieth century—the Lepines, Girerds, Bells, Turners, the Roy Blacks—my close kin, who, along with my great-grandfather and grandfather, dreamed of raising rice. They and other early rice farmers realized their dreams; DeWitt is surrounded by rice fields.

For seventeen years, until I left for college, I was a part of DeWitt. It has never left me. Despite the setbacks and losses of my adult life, I'm relatively happy, optimistic, and, on most days, sane. Luck was with me: I grew up in a way of life now essentially vanished from America, raised by parents who seemed to enjoy me, among folk who knew my name.

Garot
farmhouse

Jo on Farmall "M" tractor, Garot farm lot, c. 1940

Jo with pet chicken,
Garot farm, 1939

Jo with mother, Cousin Albert Andrews, Grandfather Jessie Butler Merritt, and father in oat field, Garot farm, 1939

Jo with Laddie at homeplace, 1939

Barn on Garot farm lot

Jo's father with Fairbanks Morse engine, c. 1960. (Photo from *Progressive Farmer*)

Pumping-plant shed, Garot farm

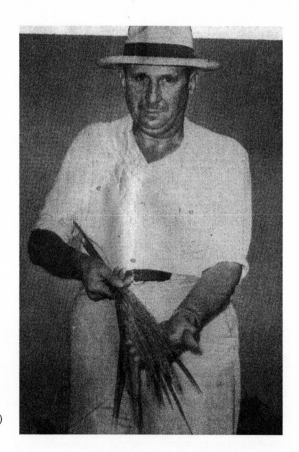

Jo's father with rice
stalks, c. 1960. (Photo
from *Progressive Farmer*)

Self-propelled combine for harvesting rice. This combine was one of the first in use on the Arkansas Grand Prairie, c. 1945. (Photo taken at Museum of the Arkansas Grand Prairie, Stuttgart)

Threshing machines were in use on Arkansas Grand Prairie rice farms from the early 1900s to the mid-1940s. (Photo taken at Museum of the Arkansas Grand Prairie, Stuttgart)

Binders were in use on Arkansas Grand Prairie rice farms from the early 1900s to the mid-1940s. (Photo taken at Museum of the Arkansas Grand Prairie, Stuttgart)

Jo and father at homeplace, 1940

Jo's parents, Leon Joseph and Ruth Maurine (Merritt) Garot, Garot farmhouse, 1934

Jo and mother, 1940

Jo and sister, Nancy, at homeplace, Flicka on the right, c. 1948

Nancy, left, with parents and Jo, at homeplace, 1960s

Jo's paternal great-grandparents, Leon Joseph and Marie Therese (Scarceriaux) Garot

Jo's paternal grandparents, Pierre (Peter) Joseph and Augusta Josephine (Fenasse)
Garot, with Leon, c. 1913

Leon with parents on camping trip, Arkansas Ozarks, 1922

Leon "ready" for the hunt, Happy Hollow, Hot Springs, c. 1918.
(Photo by Arlington Studios)

Leon with kill, early 1930s

Grandfather and Grandmother Garot with dog, Garot homeplace, mid-1930s

Grandmother
Garot, center,
and sister
Emilia Fenasse
on the right
Belgium,
c. 1952

Jo's maternal grandparents, Jessie Butler and Hattie (Harden) Merritt, at Merritt farm,
Cabot, mid-1920s

Granddad Merritt on Merritt farm, c. 1940

Jo with Granddad Merritt and Daisy, Merritt homeplace, 1939

Jo's uncle, Coy Merritt, on left, in army uniform, early 1940s

Jo and Great-aunt Alice Legg, Garot farm, 1939

Jo and Albert in Florida, c. 1940

Merritt homeplace, Ruth Merritt on porch, c. 1915

Villa Augusta with view of Lake Hamilton, Hot Springs, c. 1946

Granddad Garot at Villa Augusta, c. 1936

Jo with friend
Meredith Miller,
DeWitt, c. 1947.
(Photo courtesy of
Meredith [Miller]
Wilburn)

Jo with friend Gay Hudspeth, left, and Rusty, DeWitt, c. 1945

CHAPTER 8

Daddy

HOMEPLACE

I remember my father when I was six
pushing open the gate on the farm road,
stirring the dust of August.
The locusts sizzling in the grass,
a hum of dragonflies hanging sleepy above us.

On a Saturday in late September 1940, I'm playing hopscotch in the backyard of the house. It's absurdly hot, and I'm dressed in my favorite pink shorts and white sandals. Adjacent to the yard lies one of my father's rice fields, ready for harvest, the field I see every day from my room. Bob, the hired hand who, my father says, "hasn't got the brains God gave a goose," has bumbled a grain wagon into the field. Gone home to supper, he's forgotten to close the gate.

My dog of the moment, Laddie, a black-and-white "rat" terrier who wouldn't know a rat from a rhinoceros, moseys toward the field. He looks back, inviting me. At the age of five, I'm not hard to persuade, although

I hesitate. This field of rice, yawning in the heat, climbs higher than my head and goes on, it seems, all the way into town, maybe even across the river to Little Rock. Dad has issued me a strict warning about this: When a field of rice has grown to its mature height—as tall as my six-foot father's breast pocket—I must not, under any circumstances, enter there. I hear his voice in my head: "You get in that field of rice when it's grown, it'll swallow you up. You'll be gone in no time. We'll never find you."

Whistling "You Are My Sunshine," I follow Laddie into the field. My mother's house dwindles behind me. I enter a Black Forest of rice, its odor a mix of drying hay and just-baked pie crust. The crickets have begun the singing that I'll come to associate with graves. I push on, following Laddie's exuberant lead. A red-winged blackbird balances on a rice stalk, bending it almost to the ground.

The blackbird makes one or two of its piercing calls and flies away. Then, silence. The rice closes its ranks over and around me. I've lost sight of Laddie in the dusk. Above, ahead, beside, behind me lurk nothing but rice stalks, each one a clone of the other, impersonal and banal. A rustle, a message in code, speeds like brushfire through the grain.

Through the patchy ceiling of rice, the last of daylight descends as if through water; a sliver of a moon appears. I am drowning. I want my mother. I want my room. Something nudges my foot. My heart rattles up past my collarbone.

"Jo! Jo Hamel!" Someone calls from a great distance, using both my given names, a guarantee of trouble. "Jo! Answer me. You answer me right now, young lady, you hear?" Daddy. I don't want to be left in the coming dark, abandoned to this lock-step army of rice; I want even less to face my father. I say nothing. Laddie, having circled back to me, says nothing. Dad calls again, harsher, closer. "Answer me, young lady!" Then I see, just above the rice stalks, a straw fedora skimming along, no visible body or face beneath it.

My father looms like Colossus in front of me. In Vacation Bible School, I've seen a picture of the sea parted by Moses; Dad's face grows darker than that water. "You. Turn. Around. Right. Now," he says. "And you head for home." I hear the relief in his voice, but I feel the willow switch on my bare legs, little stinging swipes every step of the three or four decades it takes to get to my mother's house. "Didn't I tell you? And you went in that field anyway? Don't you ever, ever do that again," he says, punctuating every other word with the switch. "You hear?" The air has cooled; the rice has grown aloof, bereft now of crickets and blackbirds and light. Tail down, Laddie tucks in beside me, headed home.

———

It's late March, 1985. We've just left Mother's new grave. From the front living room of my mother's house, if the draperies were open—and, as usual, they're not—I could see the rice field in which I once was lost and terrified. Placid now, ready for planting, its plowed dirt shines like taffeta. The side yard where my father tried to teach me to bat a softball, where I once stepped barefoot on a toad, offers up its usual miserly grass. Long shadows decimate the hen house, the chicken coops, the dry stalks in Mother's garden.

My father, my sister, and I have gathered in this room, Dad in his favorite chair, a Victorian atrocity upholstered in teal blue velvet. He sits at the front of the chair, somber, cleaning his fingernails with a pocketknife. Nancy and I lean back, eyes closed, waiting. The three of us find ourselves alone for the first time since Mother's last, blurred days in the hospital. Numb from the swirls of people milling through the house, the tumbling light and sounds and despair of the funeral, I feel as stoic as the woman in *American Gothic*. Dad snaps shut his knife and sighs. "Girls, you're not to move anything in this house," he announces, in the same imperious way he used to tell Nancy or me the exact time to be home after a date. "You understand? Nothing."

My sister and I exchange looks. The two-story house we'd grown up in is overstuffed with things. The china cabinets in the dining room have gone berserk with china and silver; I can't remember when their doors would fully shut. In Mother's closets, the dresses and blouses and pants enjoy a distressing intimacy; reaching for one dress, you'll likely get four. The sunroom, with a sea of boxes of unpacked goods from ancient auctions, has long been off-limits to pedestrians. The shelves of the room we sit in bear art glass, World's Fair spoons, old theater tickets, and thimbles. Surely no one would notice if we took a toothpick holder or a ceramic rose or even the conch shell propping open the dining-room door.

The house has been in Dad's family for three generations, but the house is unmistakably Mother's. She's embossed it with her style: the

Waterford crystal chandeliers, the baroque plantation mirrors, the his-and-hers guest towels, the fake Tiffany and genuine cut glass.

The afternoon has disappeared. In the milky gloom, I can scarcely see my sister's face. I get up to turn on a light.

"Sit down," Dad commands.

I'm glad Mother can't see this scene: Nancy and I in our stylish, funereal dresses, Daddy in the worst suit he owns, a brown one, and black vinyl boots.

"Why?" I ask.

"Because she liked it dark. Leave the light alone. Leave everything alone, I tell you."

My mother's house is dying.

———

The next day arrives in a stupor of heat. Nancy has gone back to Edgemont, but I'll stay a while. On spring break from teaching, I don't have to be back in Kansas for a week. I'm hoping to help my father find a shape for his life. He doesn't find it while I visit; at his death, nine years later, he still will not have found it. My mother absconded with his reason for living.

The radio in the kitchen predicts eighty-seven degrees by afternoon, too warm for March, even in Arkansas. Preparing breakfast for Daddy, I can't find anything I need. I look for a skillet in the stove's warming drawer; I find mouse droppings and two marbles.

Dad comes downstairs. "What are you doing?" he says, alarmed at see-ing me riffling through the cabinets. I search for a place on the chrome-trimmed dinette table to set his breakfast plate, finally settling for the top of a Bible. No less than eight, some still in boxes, grace the table, sharing it with a bowl of wax pears.

I concoct breakfast. Dad smears egg around his plate and hands it back to me without a word. "Daddy," I remind him, "we've got to take all those pans and dishes back. This afternoon." He shrugs. "This after-noon," I repeat. Before Mother's funeral, friends had brought enough fried chicken, ham, meat loaf, chocolate cake, tuna casserole, apple pies, and Jell-O salads to feed all of DeWitt and half of Stuttgart. "I'll be back at eleven o'clock," he sighs. He slips on a windbreaker and his felt hat. "It's already eighty degrees out there," I protest. "You'll burn up." Head down, he strides out, muttering something about a harrow. It occurs to me I've never seen my father in short sleeves.

Dad returns in an hour, sweaty and out of sorts. We climb into his recalcitrant Buick to make our several-dozen stops. We return casserole dishes, pie tins, cake stands, plates—all marked by their owners with red nail polish or adhesive strips. I recognize many of the houses; they were on Mother's milk-and-egg route some forty-five years ago. Although many of the housewives ask to see him, Daddy refuses, making himself small in the passenger seat. "I've got to get home," he protests at every stop. "I've got a tractor broke down." A headache the size of a dime sets up shop over my left eye. "We're doing this *today*," I tell him, "no matter how long it takes."

During my short sojourn with him, Dad and I argue every day. I want some small belonging of my mother's—a piece of costume jewelry, a scarf, an empty perfume bottle, anything—to hold in my hand. He refuses. The house is completely shut to sunlight; I open the draperies, he closes them. There is not an inch of clear surface in the bathroom I am using: I have no place to put even a bobby pin. Dad inspects each room in the evenings to see that nothing has been moved.

Mother's presence insinuates itself everywhere: the scent of her Blue Grass cologne, the odor of mothballs in every closet, the bric-a-brac and books and hats and makeup samples and handbags. When I leave the house to go back to Kansas and my job, I take—from so far back in her closet I'm sure even my father will never notice—a pair of my mother's brown lizard high-heeled pumps.

Although I will see my father often after Mother's death, in Pittsburg or Little Rock or Kansas City, ten years and many legal impasses will assert themselves before I'll enter this house again.

The backyard has simmered to nearly one hundred degrees. My father stands with two or three men I've never seen, insurance salesmen probably. In the summer of my sixth or seventh year, happy to be out of school, I skip barefoot around the yard. I run toward Dad to tell him the cat has once again messed in the sandbox.

I don't see the toad. Cold and yielding, primeval and wrong, it fits itself under the arch of my right foot. Terror takes over my eyes, my fingers, my ears, my blood. The world vanishes; everything turns black; I will never reach my father. I fling myself at him, screaming, and deadlock my arms around his waist. Although Daddy doesn't suffer cowards gladly, this time he doesn't scold. "It's okay, Puddin'," he says, hugging me close. "It's okay." I smell the sunlight in his shirt. He swabs at my tears with a white handkerchief that smells reassuringly of bleach. "It's okay now; it's just a frog," he says, dispatching the monster over the fence. I marvel at how tall my father is, how fierce, how he blocks the sun.

———

As a farmer, Dad presented a paradox of both convention and daring. When he bought the self-propelled combine at the end of World War II, he stepped out as one of the first farmers in Arkansas County to do so. It was fiery red, an International Harvester. I was ten and inordinately proud. Other farmers were coming to view this curious piece of equipment. My father was being recognized as a progressive player in the business.

The combine was revolutionary, performing the tasks of two machines: the binder and the threshing machine. One combine performed the tasks of dozens of men. It cut the rice, separated the grain from the stalks, and augured it into trucks for transport to the mill. Now, with a combine and minimal crew, a farmer could harvest a small field in one day instead of weeks—a boon in an industry joined at the hip to the weather.

Tilting through fields with all the finesse of a dinosaur, the combine marked a sea change in the agricultural world. The machines it replaced, however—the binder and the threshing machine—also had caused waves in their day, supplanting the handheld scythe and rake. Now progress, relentlessly unfaithful, had deemed the combine its momentary star. I felt a twinge of regret for the threshing machine and the binder, those icons of power and swagger as I was growing up.

Invented by Cyrus McCormick, the binder was drawn by mules or a tractor. It cut the grain with a sickle bar and, in a series of ingenious steps, secured it with twine into bundles—no more laborious gleaning and binding stalks of grain by hand. The human element was still in evidence, however. As the bundled grain tumbled from the binder onto the ground, it was gathered up by "shockers," men who moved deftly through the fields, propping bundles of rice against each other to make shocks. When the shockers were finished, the fields were punctuated with myriads of dun-colored teepees.

When I was a child, harvest began in September; with it often came the rain. Needing two or three weeks to cure, vulnerable to moisture, shocks languishing in the field caused my father endless worry. Rot and sprouting became his harvest demons.

When the rice was finally cut and hauled from the fields to the threshing machine, my father breathed easier. Until usurped by the combine, the threshing machine had been revered, a giant step up from flailing grain by hand. Powered by a steam-driven, stationary tractor, the unsightly machine held high court at harvest, its only duty to stand in one spot and wait for its rations of rice.

The rice arrived on carts known as bundle wagons. I faintly remember the wagons being drawn by horses—my father had no patience with mules—but later they were hitched to tractors. Swaying and creaking, they faced uneven rice stubble, mud, and implacable levees to make their deliveries. Having accepted the rice, the threshing machine, in a series of grudging steps akin to moving a ship through locks, sorted the hulls from the grain.

My main interest in this enterprise lay in the clouds of chaff belching from the imperious machine, adding to an ever-increasing stash on the ground of hulls, straw, detritus, and sticks. Although it was technically a straw stack, we called it a haystack, and it loomed taller every harvest, eventually accomplishing a height of twenty feet or more. This became, in warm weather, my solitary playground. Never did it occur to me that I might fall through the unstable straw and smother. Although occasionally a nest of red ants lay in ambush, I wouldn't be deterred from slogging daily to the top and bumping slowly, deliciously down.

———

Harvest was, and is, a maze of highly coordinated, risk-ridden tasks. Every harvest confounded my father with the threat of bad weather, lost time, and diffident crews. In the midst of the fray, Dad was the CEO. Everywhere at once, on foot or in his pickup, he chastised and encouraged the men, cleared jams or "choke-ups" in the binder, cursed every breakdown, and slammed the pickup back and forth to town for parts.

Because of the lurching machinery, driven by men with seemingly no peripheral vision, I was barred from the fields at harvest. If, however, I promised to stay out of the way, I was allowed on the edge of the threshing lot. The noise was overwhelming; I understood almost nothing, technically, of what was going on; and no one had time for me. Still, I was fascinated with this bristling panorama—the ferment and hope, the mystery, the general, prevailing chaos. I was learning, too, the peculiar vocabulary of farming—the lean sounds and forthright images that, in naming things, explain them. Watching from my protected spot at the edge, I thought harvest was exotic.

Harvest lasted, in those days, from September until Thanksgiving or later. My father would clump into the house sometimes as late as ten P.M. for supper, having mined the last vestige of daylight. Grimy, emptying grains of rice from his pants cuffs, Dad was agitated on a good day, inconsolable on a bad one. A farmer lives always with impending doom, gambling everything, every year, on the crop. Harvest is the cautionary joy, the reward. Or not.

I must have been four or five the year that, for my father, it was not. Slumped at the kitchen table one evening in 1939 or 1940, Dad announced to Mother that the rice, "the whole damn crop," had been hit by "white tip." Sitting between my parents—who seemed to have forgotten me—I had no idea what white tip was. I thought of Laddie's white-tipped tail. Was my dog somehow to blame? Despair filled the room like a slowly rising river. My father paced the kitchen, sighing, predicting a "hard winter," hands deep in his pockets. Hearing the words "crop failure," I was terrified. I asked Daddy, my heart racing, "Are we going to be poor?"

"No . . . I hope not . . . I don't know," he said, looking at Mother. "But we're going to have to hunker down."

What did that mean? Nothing to wear? Nothing to eat? Maybe I'd have to get rid of Laddie. I hurried outside, finding the dog asleep, nonchalant at the back door.

Dad garnered a yield that year, though small. White tip, a disease that prevents grain from forming in the husk, producing "blanks," took its toll. Still, my father made a crop. When things looked bleak—a late planting, a still-later harvest, low prices, too much rain or not enough—my father would say, eventually and philosophically, "We'll make a crop. We always do. We've never not made a crop." Years afterward, on our own farm, I was to hear my husband repeat that mantra, and, later, our son.

I was witness to agricultural history as the self-propelled combine quickly displaced the threshing machine and binder, sentinels of my childhood. The combine meant fewer men, more machines; thinner payrolls, fatter profit. Regretfully, it also requisitioned a colorful part of my world.

The hoboes who came around at every harvest gradually disappeared, and with them their stories, their rowdy talk, their aura of a distant, forbidden way of life. By the time I turned eleven, Buck, missing all his teeth, was gone, as well as the young, blond migrant who drew pictures of horses for me on cast-off boards.

I missed them. I missed, too, going through the woods with my father—which I had done since I was five—to round up threshing crews from such towns as Tichnor and Nady, communities lying south and east of DeWitt. Close to the White River National Wildlife Refuge, many of these settlements were no more than crossroads, some with a small church, all with modest houses dwarfed by giant trees. Rice fields threatened to invade the towns. Shade and a modicum of coolness existed there, even in late August, when Dad began assembling his workers.

Daddy stops the pickup near a monstrous oak that hovers over the house beneath it. Sunlight fights its way through the canopy. Gradually, we've come off the nearly treeless landscape around our farm into an abundance of trees, perhaps a forest. Even before Dad shuts off the pickup, a man comes to stand on the house steps, his hands in his pockets.

"Wait here," Daddy says to me. "I'll be back in a minute."

My father walks toward the man, who grudgingly moves down from the steps. Dad doesn't offer to close the distance between them; he waits for the man to come to him. They chat briefly, the man never looking up from the ground, nodding now and then at something my father says.

There's no birdsong, no bark of a dog, just the presence of these ancient trees and the occasional sound of a leaf falling to the ground. Civilization seems hundreds of miles away. I've heard of panthers in these woods, their shrieks sounding like a woman's scream.

I can't make out the conversation going on a few yards in front of the pickup, but judging from his air of indifference, the man has heard my father's pitch before. I know not to get out of the truck. This is between men.

Dad returns to the pickup. "Well," he says with a mix of exasperation and relief, "I guess he'll come around. He's not the best shocker in the world, but he'll have to do."

With the advent of the combine, traditions were erased. Not only were we bereft of the hoboes, but we lost the threshing machine that Daddy would throw his hat into, as his father had done before him, on the last day of harvest. And there was no more haystack—regal, burnished yellow, and glistening with promise, smelling the way cognac looks.

Dad soon reverted to his old ways, eschewing new equipment for used. The red combine faded, grew obsolete, and was consigned to harboring weeds until it was auctioned off some fifty years later.

By the time of the machinery and equipment auction, held to expedite the settlement of Dad's estate, the farm lot had become an ode to inertia, decay, and my father's helpless loyalty to his father and grandfather, farmers before him. Seemingly incapable of discarding anything they'd ever owned, Dad simply left their possessions where they stood: a vintage bob truck, antique disks, tractors, harrows, and plows. Sentiment, fear, and unbridled space turned both my mother and father into consummate pack rats.

Little was ever thrown or given away—neither burlap bag nor string nor rotted lumber nor new appliances still in their unopened crates. During the six or seven auctions of personal and farm goods, I marveled, ashamed, at the waste.

At one of these auctions, however—the one in which I tried unsuccessfully to regain the red wagon—I was happy for my father's obsession with the past. He had kept, still in its station near the weir pond, the one-and-a-half-story Fairbanks Morse engine I'd listened to night after night. Made of dull black steel and weighing approximately two tons, the Fairbanks, as Dad liked to call it, had long been replaced by a more efficient, compact power unit. Nevertheless, when I was a child, the Fairbanks had been the force that powered the pump that watered the rice—making it, in spring and summer, king of the farm.

I'd regarded the massive engine in those days with a mixture of resentment, awe, and fear. Arrogant as a cottonmouth, the Fairbanks exuded an air of stolid aggressiveness. Certainly it commanded my father's respect and attention, as it had my grandfather's, who'd built a protective shed (known as the pumping shed) for it. The shed also housed the treacherous, long belt that transmitted power from the engine to the pump.

The Fairbanks was a prima donna. It needed servicing every four or five hours. It would shut down if exposed to extreme cold or heat. The belt often would come loose and the engine "run away" with itself.

When the Fairbanks engine missed or stopped, my father would jolt out of sleep or flee the breakfast table or stop dead in midsentence to scramble to the pumping shed. Starting the engine was a complicated procedure involving at least two men, a flywheel, compressed air, infinite patience, and as much as half a day. Meanwhile, my father would fume. If the Fairbanks stayed down too long, the rice would suffer, starved for water.

Because of the near-constant maintenance required, it was customary to hire a man, usually young and single, to live beside the engine. Dad hired Virgil, even though Virgil wasn't single; he and Loretta came as newlyweds to the shed that had been furnished with a cot, a splintery counter, and a hot plate. Noise from the engine made talk impossible, but Loretta invited me for cookies every afternoon.

Almost all the neighboring farms boasted Fairbanks Morse or Bessemer engines. Operating at a slow 600 rpm, these behemoths provided, in noisy and mostly unerring iambic pentameter, the collective heartbeat of the Grand Prairie. When the Fairbanks was happy, its resonant, thick sound could be heard for a quarter of a mile. Our engine stood behind the house, scarcely two hundred yards from my open bedroom window. On summer evenings, the sound of it seeped into my sleep.

This engine was the pulse of our lives. Its start-up each spring brought promise: There would be water, abundant rice, a crop. We would not go without.

———————

Although it's early morning, perhaps eight o'clock, the summer heat has already stilled the sparrows. "Stay close to the wall, now," Dad commands, frowning. "Don't get anywhere near that belt." He grips my hand. "Stay right beside me." My father has to shout to be heard. He's come to service the Fairbanks, which swallows every sound except its own.

Six or seven years old, I've wheedled Dad into letting me come along. We're in the long, narrow part of the T-shaped shed that houses the Fairbanks engine and the dreaded belt. Hugging one side of the shed as we walk along, we keep our distance from the belt, forty feet of relentless speed. The heat, coupled with the friction of working machinery, has turned the tin-roofed shed into a furnace fit for Shadrach, Meshach, and Abednego. The vibration of the mammoth engine invades my ears, my chest, my eyes, my feet.

Finished with his inspection, Daddy steers me quickly outside.

"Why'd we have to stay so close to the wall?" I ask. "Because," my father sighs, offering his usual one-word answer. His voice goes dark, as if a late-summer shower were gathering in it. "Listen," he says. "You're never to go in that shed by yourself. You hear?" Taking a handkerchief from his back pocket, he wipes the sweat from his eyes. "If you're pulled in by that belt, you're done for. Nobody can save you." He folds and tucks the handkerchief into its pocket. "You wouldn't even have time to scream."

What my father feared was the violent draft created by the lightning-swift belt, a draft that could fluff out a shirttail or a sleeve, snatching it instantly. An arm or hand would surely be lost then, quite probably a life.

My father tried to protect me not only from the dangers of the pumping shed but also from other violence on the farm, usually concerning the animals. When the cattle were branded each year, I was not allowed near the pen. When my father went out one stormy spring night to help a cow with a breech delivery, I was, despite my begging to go with him, ordered to bed.

When Dad couldn't shield me completely, he was usually honest in answering my questions. Fluffy, the dog who followed Laddie in my affections, disappeared one fall day. When I asked my father where she was, Dad said she'd most likely been shot by a hunter. Stunned, I asked why. "Well," he said, hesitating, "some people just shoot dogs for the fun of it." I was devastated, but heartened by my father's treating me as an adult, old enough to hear the truth.

The human face of danger, I soon learned, didn't confine itself to random shooters of dogs. My first, fearful introduction to the mysteries of the opposite sex occurred one day when a boy, the son of one of the hired men, looked at me in a knowing way, suggesting things I didn't, at nine or ten, understand. I repeated them to my mother, who surely told my father, who, undoubtedly, spoke to the hired man. Although the man continued to work sporadically for Dad, I never saw the boy on the farm again.

———

Like most farmers, Dad counted danger as his daily companion. When I was very young, he told me of witnessing a man killed when the tractor he was driving overturned on a steep bank, pinning the man beneath it. Dad came home saying the man had no burial insurance; I was perplexed, hearing it as "barrel" insurance.

Dad had seen fingers given up to augers. Respectful of moving cogs and chains, he never wore rings, not even his wedding band. He had, in his early days of farming, barely escaped a deadly tornado, and he was vigilant about lightning and its attraction, in an open field, to metal shovels.

As if to offset the harshness of the farm, Dad also emphasized its wonders. Once he brought me a passel of baby rabbits whose nest he'd disturbed while plowing. I fed them from a doll's bottle. One winter, taking advantage of a rare, thunking freeze, Dad took me skating on the weir pond. He granted my collection of small green box turtles docking space in the watering trough, and each Christmas season, Dad and I solemnly cut the tree, a cedar we would find somewhere on the farm. It was family tradition to have the tree in the house by my December birthday.

My father loved the smell of dirt, familiar and jarring. He liked the shine of it in spring, the silky dust of it in summer, its bland, winter bleakness. He liked to hold it in his hands. He breathed it. He seemed to will it into his bones.

Once in early spring, before plowing, Dad and I took a sack lunch into a field near the house. A full-canopied oak stood close to the field's center. Although a bother to tractors and other machinery, it had been spared; Dad never said why. He insisted we sit under the tree, on the barely thawed ground. We ate our sandwiches, observing the running clouds. In a little while, I declared, apropos of nothing and with all the wisdom of my five or six years, "The clouds are angels." Daddy took another bite of Vienna sausage. "I'll bet you're right, Podunk." He studied the clouds intently, as if he'd lost a calf in their midst. "They're angels, all right," he concurred, nodding. "Sure as I'm sitting here." I went home smug as a senator.

———

The men who'd helped Dad plow this field, mend its fences, and shovel its levees—the hired hands—stand, then and now, as the overlooked heroes of the rice industry. Almost never identified in photo captions, these men provided the hard labor and scalding-hot, mosquito-ridden hours to put in and harvest a crop. Poorly educated as a rule in the 1940s, living almost always on poverty's embankment, sunburned, chronically in need of dental work, these men knew the farms they worked on intimately, having shoveled every levee of every field. In one of my father's ledgers from 1944, he's entered countless payments due him from Bill, my wagon-pulling buddy, for an ongoing car loan.

Conditions have improved somewhat for hired men on today's farms, but still they often go unnamed in photographs.

———

With us all the years I can remember, Bill corners my father as he's coming from a field toward the house. The farm lurches in the pell-mell, double-time tempo before harvest; it's mercilessly hot even in the shade of the elm, where Bill has waited for at least an hour. He leans heavily on his levee shovel as he talks. Playing in the washhouse, I'm not close enough to hear all of what is said, and it's not a conversation exactly, more a one-man show by Bill, who's likely informing my father of a heifer's sore hoof or a rotting plank in the barn, or his sick wife, for which he needs a loan to pay the doctor. Bill leans farther in to Daddy, gesturing often and urgently. My father says little, half turning toward the house again and again, where lunch is getting cold. Then he wrings his hands toward the ground once, frowning and agitated, a sign that the audience is over. Bill will be obliged to repeat this scene many times before "Mr. Leon" sees fit to fix whatever has gone wrong.

My father farmed, almost all his working life, with broken-down, jittery equipment, making few improvements to the land. At the time of his forced retirement in the early 1990s, he'd been farming almost as he had in the 1940s. "Well," he would say when someone questioned his methods, "look around you"—referring to those in the region who had lost their farms. "At least I'm still in the game."

When it came to research and invention, that is, better ways to water rice, fashion a smarter part for an ailing combine, or breed Hereford cattle—my father stepped forward, progressive and questioning and tenacious. One example is a trip he made in the mid-1940s to research rice-growing in the tropics.

I was eleven and my sister nine months old when the family boarded a United Fruit Company banana freighter in New Orleans, bound for Cuba and Guatemala. I was barely aware of our purpose for going, caught up in the bedazzle of the adventure.

Aboard ship, I never missed the loading of the bananas. Whatever port we docked in, when the fruit was lowered into the hold, I was there to witness the elaborate cacophony of nets and hooks and chains and men shouting. The odor of green bananas was shocking. Even now, seeing unripe bananas at the grocer's, the acid, too-sweet smell of tons of green bananas shoots to my brain.

Havana proved to be the liveliest city I had ever seen, topping Chicago, Miami, and San Francisco—not to mention North Little Rock.

Cuba lived then, in the late 1940s, in the pre-Castro era of Batista, of course—and in that freewheeling, corrupt world, I was allowed to do things I'd never have been granted in the States: I toured a rum factory, getting sick on the generous samples. I stepped into the color-soaked world of the Copacabana, no questions asked. Nobody looked askance when Dad took me to a cockfight just outside Havana.

Guatemala I remember most for its lush foliage—at least as green as Ireland's. Riding the train through the countryside surrounding Guatemala City, I saw poverty such as I had never witnessed. At almost every shack along the tracks, a naked toddler stood, staring, in a bare dirt yard. Some waved; some relieved themselves as we wobbled by.

———

Dad's heart, at least at first, may not have been in farming. He enjoyed the rice research he did for the Station, as the locals call it. Had my grandfather Garot not moved to Hot Springs for his health, insisting Daddy take over the farm, Dad might have chosen advanced research in rice varieties as a career.

Despite Dad's reservations about farming at the outset, he seemed to have embraced it over the years. It became not simply his occupation, but his calling. "I'll never retire," he declared vehemently when he reached his seventies and people began to suggest such heresy. "I'll die on my tractor."

I wish it could have been that way. He died in a hospital from cancer, raging and indignant. He had requested we read Tennyson's "Crossing the Bar" at his funeral and that "The Old Rugged Cross" lead the group of hymns. We included the poem, but not, to my regret, the hymn, one that I have never liked. He reproaches me for that now, head down, fedora crammed on his head, striding out through silent fields of rice.

CHAPTER 9

Where the Saltwater Can't Get at the Rice

MOTHER'S words brush my arm with foreboding like the wings of a moth. Searching the family archives for letters, I've found the one Mother gave me on July 3, 1957, before she, Dad, and Nancy traveled to Europe. Among other things, she writes of the homeplace and the farm.

> Jo,
>
> One never knows what might happen when we leave home so, if it does, remember to love and cherish this home and farm. . . . Remember Daddy & Granddaddy have worked their life away for you kids. . . .
>
> Love,
> Mother & Daddy

At the time of Mother's writing, I'm twenty-one, married, and two weeks away from delivering my firstborn, Charla. Nancy is eleven.

I'd known ever since my teenage years that Mother and Dad fervently wanted the farm to stay in the family, but until my mother's warning note, I'd given scant thought to loss, heritage, history, and my place in them. I began asking questions—not enough, I now realize—about Grandfather's journey that transformed an immigrant cabinetmaker into a farmer, bringing him to land that had known the Quapaw and the buffalo.

Daddy was my grandparents' only child, born after they adopted America. In a stoic photo of the young family, Grandfather Garot wears a three-piece suit and a tie, his eyebrows and hair black as a grizzly's. Grandmother has donned a blouse and ankle-length skirt. Dad is probably four or five at the time of this photo. He stands as still as Lot's wife. The trio could be the poster family of the 1900s: the father seated; the mother standing, one hand on her husband's shoulder; the child's hand resting lightly on his father's knee. Of course, as was the custom of the Victorian day, nobody smiles.

According to Dad, Grandmother sailed from Belgium to New Orleans to marry Grandfather, forbidden to do so by her parents, who threatened to disown her. When she ran away in 1904, she was twenty, my grandfather twenty-nine.

Granddad was barely a preteen when he left Belgium for America in 1886. In Charleroi, his father had been a coal miner, then a joiner, and fairly well-to-do. His sons—Adolph Joseph, Victor Joseph, and Pierre Joseph— were set to follow him in the custom-cabinetry trade. Something soured between the Protestant Garot family and the Catholic community, however, and gradually the work disappeared. (Adolph long maintained but could not prove that the Catholic Church in Charleroi commandeered much of the family's funds.)

Whatever the stressful cause, the clan—comprised of Great-grandfather Leon Joseph Garot, Great-grandmother Marie Therese (Scarceriaux) Garot, and seven children—decided to leave Belgium. An overriding question, of course, must have loomed: where to go? I wonder how they decided. Nine people uprooted themselves from family, friends, country, town—all that represented home. I wanted details of that road that had made all the difference. I wanted stories.

One relative remained alive who might offer them—Victor Girerd, Dad's first cousin, one year older than Dad. Victor's mother was Grandfather Garot's sister. Hoping she might have passed down family anecdotes and hoping Victor at ninety-three would remember them, I phoned him.

———

My husband and I arrive at Victor's house near DeWitt on a July day obese with heat, in 2003. As we step out of the car, the Delta light blinds us, sudden as a stroke. Charles and I, living now in Little Rock but raised in this flat country, well remember its sledgehammer heat and light.

Standing at Victor's back door, we remark that we've never entered a farmhouse through the front door except to pay condolence calls.

Victor invites us through the ragtag kitchen into the living room. A bachelor, he's lived most of his life in this house, on this farm, raising rice. Heat pillories the room; I welcome the knock and hum of a window air-conditioner. "I haven't seen you in a while," Victor says, with a familiar accent, giving a French inflection to certain words as Dad used to do. He invites us to sit, rustling into the kitchen for glasses of iced tea. I follow to help, reminding him how he used to enjoy singing in the Methodist men's Sunday-school class I played so badly for. We laugh. Victor is trim, his brown eyes alert. My husband, whose family farm lies nearby, has long admired Victor's work ethic. As Victor returns, Charles remarks on the sumptuous garden behind the house. "It used to be a real garden," Victor says, "but I've slowed down."

From my chair in the living room, I can see the clutter on the kitchen counter. Victor sits in a recliner garnished with a yellowed cotton throw. He knew my father and grandfather well; I ask him to tell what he remembers of them. "I have good memories," Victor says. He gestures toward the back door. "Your old homeplace, you know, isn't far from here. We visited Uncle Joe and Aunt Augusta every Sunday when we were kids."

As if remembering my grandparents' hospitality, Victor returns to the kitchen for paper napkins, talking as he goes. "All the cousins, we'd play in the yard. In summer it was really dusty." He returns to his chair, swatting at a mosquito. "Your dad had a dog that he pulled around the yard in a wagon." Victor smiles. "The little dog sat so still."

I tell Victor I'm looking, too, for stories of our family's journey from Belgium to Arkansas by way of Louisiana, of those days when they joined the helter-skelter land rush to the Grand Prairie.

The air conditioner stumbles and groans; the outside temperature had reached ninety-five degrees on our way to Victor's, according to the car radio. Victor pauses. "You remember Adolph, don't you?" I do. . . . Uncle Adolph, the oldest of Granddad's siblings, a white-bearded man by the time I knew him, married to Aunt Mary, famous for her filé gumbo . . .

Victor interrupts: "He was the family's adventurer, the one with the grand ideas. Possibilities—Adolph always saw the possibilities," he says in admiration. "He was just nineteen, you know, when they left Belgium." We're offered more iced tea, but Victor forgets to bring it, focused on the story. "They wanted a French-speaking city. Adolph considered North Africa, maybe Algiers." I think of the French Foreign Legion. I wonder if Grandmother would have followed my grandfather to Algiers. "Eventually," Victor says, "they settled on New Orleans."

Victor doesn't know how long the Garot clan stayed in the Crescent City, but work proved as scarce in the New World as in the Old. He pushes aside the ottoman stationed in front of his chair. "Nobody wanted the handmade trim and fine cabinets anymore," he says with a shrug. "They wanted the factory stuff. It was cheaper."

Victor pulls down a window shade against the marauding light. The room holds mismatched furniture that most likely began its tour of duty with Victor's grandmother. A 1950s TV hunkers on a table, a wilted doily beneath it. Although retired from farming, Victor invests himself in the world around him, but not so his house. The 1940s came and went, the decades moved on, but Victor's abode, like Melville's Bartleby, preferred not to.

"So how did the clan end up in Crowley?" I ask. Victor laughs. "By accident. A pastor suggested it. Crowley's not far from New Orleans, you know. He said they might find work on the rice farms." Indeed, I'd read somewhere that Crowley had been named, after the Civil War, the Rice Capital of America, a title soon to be relinquished to Arkansas itself.

Victor can't fix the exact date, but sometime in the early 1900s, after the disappointment of New Orleans and before their flight into Arkansas, the Garot clan settled in Louisiana's tiny Iota, near Crowley in Acadia Parish. Here, Victor relates, my grandfather and his brothers apprenticed themselves to the romance and heartbreak of growing rice.

"I doubt," I comment, "that any of our relatives had seen at the time so much as a stalk of rice." Victor allows that my grandfather and his brothers set about growing rice and cotton with true innocence. "The land they worked wasn't good," he says, "but your grandfather soon met a Crowley farmer, Alexander Lepine." Known locally as "Lepine," the man possessed, according to Victor, "at least some" rice-growing experience. Lepine and my grandfather formed a partnership and bought land near Crowley.

Victor leans over an arm of his chair to straighten a stack of mail-order catalogs. "Lepine, you know, also became your grandfather's brother-in-law."

Alex Lepine died when I was a child, but Aunt Lepine lived into her nineties, in a house across the field from my parents. Visiting, I never looked past her creased face. She might have told me stories, tales of mules and tornadoes and failure and courtship and rice. I never asked.

The Lepine-Garot Louisiana venture foundered in disaster sometime before 1906. Two rice crops failed in succession. Farmers both, Victor and my husband speculate why: the growing number of Louisiana farmers and their greed for the newest cash crop, the greed of rice for water, and an aquifer, exhausted, falling to below sea level. Saltwater seeped into the pumps and burned the rice at first watering. Alex and my grandfather lost, Victor says, "every last penny" of their investment.

Victor goes into the kitchen, returning with a Wal-Mart sack and a large plate. He empties some of the sack onto the plate, creating a mound of too-perfect cookies. He continues the story.

After the second crop failure, Adolph found temporary work with the railroad, stenciling Pullman-car interiors to resemble mahogany. When the job ended, the Garot brothers hired on with a Crowley sawmill. As Victor tells it, Fate was at hand and Adolph its messenger. Sent from the mill to the Cotton Belt depot to fetch a part, Adolph spotted a poster advertising land on Arkansas's Grand Prairie: "Available. Virgin. Cheap."

The poster promised excursion trains that would take prospective buyers to Arkansas for "a look." "I don't know how he managed it," Victor chuckles, "but Adolph was always a good talker. He persuaded your grandfather and Alex to get on one of those trains. The agents showed them the land at the end of the line." The year was 1906. The nineteenth century had just slipped into the twentieth; World War I had not yet begun; and the brothers-in-law must have heard the Sirens' call. They sold their Crowley acreage, bought the land near DeWitt, and moved to Arkansas.

The rest of the family came later, except for the youngest brother, Victor (for whom my cousin is named). "He died in Iota," his namesake says. "Sunstroke. In a rice field. He was only in his twenties."

By 1914, Victor surmises, all the clan had settled in and around DeWitt. They followed my grandfather Garot, my great-uncles Alex Lepine and Adolph, and hundreds of other farmers who'd joined a new Gold Rush, the rush for rice.

According to Victor, many of the early arriving clan crowded into "one big house" once in Arkansas County. In 1909, after Dad was born—and, I imagine, at Grandmother's insistence—my grandfather began work on the house that, at this writing, stands on the farm and is over one hundred years old. My father, then my sister and I, would grow up there. Like numerous old farmhouses in the area, the house sits empty, contending with a hangdog roof and disinterested paint.

———

Kodak photos of Grandfather—taken with Grandmother and Dad on a Colorado camping trip, with friends on a deer hunt in the Arkansas "scatters," with other shooters, holding up a largesse of dead mallards—reveal a gregarious man, pleased by rare leisure time. Distressingly, however, I've found no letters, journals, or photos to shed light on Granddad's adventures in farming rice. What were his hopes, despairs, battles, fears? Perhaps in his eyes the day-to-day sowing and reaping didn't warrant comment. By the time I came to know him, Grandfather had eschewed farming for fishing on Arkansas's Lake Hamilton.

Nor did I find any accounts of the Garots crossing the Atlantic for America, although one story of the journey exists in the family lore: Someone on the ship gave the clan a grapefruit. None of them had ever tasted a grapefruit; experiencing the bitter taste, they feared they'd been poisoned.

By anecdotal account, Grand Prairie's pioneer rice farmers faced massive challenges, the ubiquitous prairie grass topping the list. My husband says his father and grandfather—who bought land near Stuttgart, coming from Chicago on an excursion train—often recalled "breaking the prairie out of sod." They burned the grass, plowed it under, wore out horses and mules using a "prairie breaker" or sod-bottom plow. The soil slopped into bog when it rained, especially in fields harboring buffalo wallows. My husband remembers his father telling of laying fence posts in the mud to help horses and steam-engine tractors pull out of a field.

Farmers who traded mule power for steam tempted another hazard —fire. My father-in-law, so I'm told, once caught his neighbor's rice field on fire with a steam-engine cinder. It was harvest time; the neighbor sued. Once, after a particularly trying year, Dad McDougall's father advised him to "trade the farm for a yellow dog, shoot the dog, and come back to Chicago."

Hardships notwithstanding, most of the early farmers prospered, finding the dirt almost embarrassingly rich. In *Beginnings of the Rice Industry in Arkansas,* a lively documentation of the early rice boom on the Grand Prairie, farmer and writer J. M. Spicer recounts a popular saying: "All you have to do is tickle this land . . . and it will laugh a crop of rice." Virgin ground and ample water, "land that had never been touched by a plough and a lake of water underneath that could not be pumped dry," offered to the early growers almost endless possibility freighted with adventure. Having begun in 1897, rice farming on the Grand Prairie had powered itself into "big business" by 1904, according to Spicer, himself a respected rice grower who had come to Stuttgart from Ohio on the Cotton Belt Railway when he was nine, traveling with his family in a rented boxcar. Two years later, in 1906, my grandfather found his way to Arkansas and higher ground—a place, he's reported to have said, "where the damned saltwater can't get at the rice."

Granddad entered the wash of speculation and greed surrounding rice that swept the southeast corner of Arkansas. Promotional posters such as the one that snagged Adolph appeared in public buildings like fleas. Prospective buyers—mostly from the Midwest—descended by rail onto the Grand Prairie, their fares waived "if they bought land," according to Spicer. "By the time of World War One," Spicer tells us, "plantings of rice in Arkansas had reached a figure of 150,000 acres." My grandfather Garot's holdings were part of those acres.

Boom time had hit Arkansas. The wonder crop attracted visionaries such as this would-be rice farmer who writes, in 1925, after seeing his first rice crop on the Grand Prairie: "What a beautiful sight! A large field of the finest grain . . . ready for harvest. . . . I was reminded of the paragraph in the Old Bible where it says, 'In that day the young men shall dream dreams and the old men prophesy.' I was neither young nor old but I dreamed dreams." Certainly Grandfather, trying again with a crop that had twice betrayed him, dreamed dreams. He must have been drawn not only to the hope of profit but also to the challenge and satisfaction of growing rice—"one of the best cereals known to man . . . which more than half the people of the world use as their principal food." (At this date, I believe that figure is closer to two-thirds.)

———

Part of what makes rice farming colorful lies in the descriptive, often wry names given to varieties of rice. Granddad Garot benefited early on from lines perfected in Louisiana, but by the late 1920s, he likely used varieties developed at the Rice Branch Experiment Station near Stuttgart.

Varieties carried the names of their countries of origin, the wives or daughters of their developers, or their edifying qualities: Jap, Honduras, Lady Wright, Edith, Storm Proof, Early Prolific, or—my favorite— Mortgage Lifter, all introduced, according to Spicer, "prior to or shortly after World War One." An early variety, Blue Rose, named for the rare blue rose that florists spent years perfecting, was most likely the name of the rice I was lost in that summer day, following my dog.

Zenith succeeded Blue Rose. Perfected at the Station from strains of Blue Rose grown on the Glen Alter farm (site of my first sewing lessons), the much-heralded Zenith found its way to growers in 1936. My father may well have worked on its development. Zenith later fell out of the picture, plagued by the dreaded white tip.

Of course, growing up, I knew nothing of the complexities of research and development, but the names of varieties intrigued me. I heard them from seed dealers, hired hands, and my father, all talking over my head. I remember one seed dealer talking with Dad about a variety called Prolific. Before I knew what "prolific" meant, I sensed it implied something good, since Daddy kept nodding in approval.

———

As late afternoon slips into Victor's living room, he continues his recollections of my grandfather Garot, praising him as a clever man as well as an accomplished surveyor. According to Victor, Granddad traveled to California during the Depression to do custom-survey work. "He carried a pistol," Victor said, "in case tramps tried to hold him up when he got off the train." My father revered Granddad's surveying equipment, packed in a handsome mahogany case. He allotted it a place of honor beside the dining-room sideboard. Dad himself practiced the art of surveying: sighting and marking lines for pulling levees in the rice fields. Properly placed, the levees assured that the rice received throughout any given field the crucial, just-right depth of water.

Sunlight, filtered through the leaves of a pin oak, toys with my shoes. I feel a moment of grace, a connectedness with my history I couldn't have known at twenty-one. Charles and I rise to go. Victor takes my hand. "I miss your dad. And my brothers and sisters. Everybody's gone except me." Victor died three years after our visit, at ninety-six.

———

In his farming career, Grandfather Garot witnessed the tractor usurping the mule, the farm truck replacing the wagon, and gravel replacing mud on farm roads to the mills. As did my father after him, Granddad saw the desperation for food—the legacies of both world wars—increase his profits. With relatives in Belgium, this no doubt caused him conflict. He died in 1947, some sixty years after finding his place in jostling America.

I wonder—what of my grandmother's adventures? I've found no documentation for Grandmother's views on her contentious journey to America, no diaries, no letters to or from her parents in Charleroi—only Christmas cards from her sisters, tied with a satin ribbon. What did she think of this bewildering country she'd come to as a bride? She scarcely spoke the language, rice fields crowded the house, and the Delta heat wrapped her like a sari.

Despite all this, I surmise Grandmother Garot was much in love with my grandfather. In April of 1933, Grandmother writes from DeWitt an empathetic note to her future daughter-in-law in Jacksonville. (My future parents are by now students at the university, of course; I imagine they're both visiting their respective parents over spring break.) "Garot," Grandmother explains, wouldn't be coming to see his betrothed over the weekend, choosing to "stay home, believe it or not." "Don't be to sad about it," Grandmother continues. "Of course I understand [your feelings] very well. While some folks forget how crazy they were, I can't forget my time. . . . I do have to admit I had a hard case."

Deeply in love or not, my grandmother had to contend with one of the Delta's worst drawbacks, the mosquito. Wherever rice is grown, it shall follow as the night the day that there will be mosquitoes. They breed in stagnant water, and rice stands in stagnant water for most of its growing season. The mosquito divines human hide like a water witch. With a snout sharp as an acupuncture needle, it draws its victim's blood, often gorging itself until it can't fly. Mosquitoes revel in the cool of early morning and evening, but even at high noon there's no escaping their nasal whine—a frenzy of sound, like a colony of maggots suddenly given voice.

Family legend has it that my grandmother once locked herself in the bedroom for a day, refusing to come out, certain she had smallpox. "Dad finally convinced her," my father said, "that her 'pox' was the mosquito. She was covered solid in bites."

———

Congenial, generous with a hand up, Grandfather Garot had a bevy of friends. Father-son relations, however, may have hit an occasional snag. My grandfather was chronically ill, traveling often to Memphis for treatment, requiring my father to drive him. Grandfather's decision, at the age of fifty-nine, to retire to Hot Springs, leaving the farming operation to my father, surely caused conflict. Nevertheless, Dad was a farmer's son, expected by his parents and the culture to succeed his father on the farm. Daddy resigned his research job in 1936 and moved his family into the farmhouse. He was twenty-five; I was one year old.

Despite occasional difficulties in their relationship, Granddad and my father kept a lively correspondence going while Dad was at the university. In 1932, before my father had met my mother, Grandfather writes from DeWitt, dispensing advice in affairs of the heart and gossip. (Although well read and fairly well educated, my grandfather, in his writing, often disallowed the rules of grammar and punctuation.)

"My Dear Boy," he writes, "I am so glad you are all right and keep ahead with your work, that['s] the way to do . . . so long you do your best, and above all take care of yourself because I dont know what I would do if you would be sick." Grandfather advised that Dad "buy some fruit."

Addressing my father's anxiety over a romantic relationship, Grandfather advises, "If she dont love you enough like you said she ought [leave] you alone." He comments on the woman and others of her family working at "the Bank," observing, "They lucky they are all working by this time of [the] Depression." Granddad continues with the latest gossip, about a young man who "got married Saturday night . . . and Monday morning the marchal took him in jail." The man bought chickens, Granddad reports, "out in the country and gave check without nothing behind them not a cent in the bank."

Grandfather winds down the letter with a rant about young people, how they "don't see no farther than their nose" and "bring grief" to their parents, concluding, "Lord I don't see how people can live that way. . . . With lots love, Dad and Mother."

Of the several letters exchanged between my grandfather and Dad, this is the one my father evidently prized, folding it around a photo of a woman not my mother, tucking it into his daybook where he budgeted the cost of textbooks and the occasional apple or pear.

After moving to Lake Hamilton, Grandfather visited the farm less and less, perhaps not wanting to be in the way. His journey had led him to his place in the American sun, a place where saltwater couldn't wreak its havoc. With wisdom and compassion, Granddad would leave it to my young father to honor, keep, and cherish that place—in his own way, in his own time.

CHAPTER 10

Villa Augusta

WHEN my grandfather Garot left the farm for an undeveloped lot near Hot Springs, he entered the over-the-top, boisterous culture of a tourist town to surpass all tourist towns. By 1936, when my paternal grandparents built their cottage beside Lake Hamilton—naming it Villa Augusta in honor of Grandmother—the city had cobbled a history of welcome for the poor and the princely, the crooked and the straight.

"Big Doc," the "Nation's Oldest Alligator!," lived there. Al Capone strutted through in the 1920s, continuing to visit until his incarceration in 1931, four years before I was born. The alligators were housed on the widely touted Gator Farm; Capone favored the Arlington, an imposing, rococo hotel under which, it was rumored, tunnels had been dug for the Mob's convenience.

Folk of all stripe trekked to the Spa City to "take the baths" at Bathhouse Row, a series of sumptuous Edwardian bathhouses dating from the early 1900s. My grandfather was among the pilgrims, hoping to cure a chronic stomach ailment; indeed, the city's healing springs were one reason he'd chosen the area for retirement. The bathhouses, marching disdainfully along Central Avenue, made ominous, luxurious, and often baffling claims: "Swedish mechanical massage and electric department." "Tubs of solid marble imbedded in marble floor." "Vapors of marble and copper in same room as tub."

Visiting my father's parents began, as did the visits to my maternal grandparents, when I was four or five. Hot Springs proved a tantalizing contrast to the farm—a delicious combination of sleaze and mountain charm. I was seduced by the city's hoopla, especially the extravagant ads for its steaming, medicinal waters. Proprietors of one of the springs declared it "the world's hottest! 147° F!" Owners of such springs as the Maurice, Big Iron, and Radio Magnesia boasted of treating rheumatism, malaria, dyspepsia, "nerves," and excessive uric acid. They made their pitch in colorful signage along every major street.

Native Americans had referred to this area in the Ouachita Mountains as "The Valley of the Vapors." In partaking of the waters, my grandfather joined a line of notables including Babe Ruth, Andrew Carnegie, Wyatt Earp, Hernando de Soto, and Billy Sunday. I think my grandmother, on the other hand, never entered a bathhouse.

Each time I visited Hot Springs, I nagged my grandparents to let me take the baths. They demurred, saying I was too little. I suspect the bathhouse was Grandfather's haven, and he preferred to go there unencumbered.

I saw Big Doc, the other main attraction in Hot Springs at the time, only once. I was probably six. With other spectators at the Gator Farm, my grandparents and I crowded around Big Doc's walled pit. Awakened from his nap, he lurched straight toward me—all scales, tail, teeth, and alleged seven hundred pounds. I was terrified. According to the establishment's banners, Big Doc lived with "1,499 other alligators brought direct from the Everglades of Florida!" These, however, were merely the chorus for the star.

Big Doc shared the spotlight with a merman, dead and pickled— "Captured in the gulf of Tonquin . . . 500 miles from Hong Kong!" The merman was shriveled, shoe-polish brown, his mouth twisted as if in disdain, his eyes red as Satan's. I stood at the glass case, believing. I resented Grandfather all afternoon for disabusing me of my illusions.

The Mob controlled the Oaklawn race track, the casinos, and essentially the town. Lucky Luciano, Meyer Lansky, and Frank Costello were frequent visitors in the 1920s and 1930s. They glittered among the town's attractions. In the course of my annual weeklong stays, my grandparents occasionally took me to lunch at the Arlington, but so far as I know, we never saw any gangsters. Grandmother seemed disappointed by the lack of criminals in the dining room, as if she'd paid for something she hadn't gotten. I didn't much care, always glad when we returned home to the cottage so I could stroll along the lake, dreaming dreams.

———

I'm seven in July of 1943, a graduate of the second grade. Daddy has brought me to Hot Springs for my yearly, brief stay with my grandparents Garot. He brings in my suitcase, takes a perfunctory look at the lake, and visits quickly with his parents. Reminding me to "be a good girl, now," he leaves: It's a long drive, he says, three hours, and he's got to be going.

My grandparents' cottage smells of mold, the lake, and tobacco. It's compact—nothing like my parents' spacious house. Grandmother consigns the villa's largest room, the glassed-in sleeping porch, to me. She scoots an army cot into position directly under a window. "The better," she proposes, "to catch the moon." In the stingy closet, wire hangers natter as I hang up my clothes. Homesickness flickers in my stomach, quick as a minnow.

On this visit, I'm troubled. I cheated on Mrs. Miles's spelling test last spring, and guilt grinds into my skin, relentless as measles. I'm troubled, too, by my parents' quarrels. I notice that my grandparents Garot laugh a lot; they smile at each other's stories. Shouldn't I be able to make my parents smile a little more? I step out onto the portico to make sure the lake is still there.

———

My grandparents began retirement in 1936 with their customary optimism and verve. Granddad was sixty-one, grandmother fifty-two. Lake Hamilton scarcely had been filled when Grandfather acquired a lot with a promised lake view, bought a fishing boat and outboard motor, and absented himself from the farm.

Granddad transformed the lot with rosebushes, ivy, and blooming perennials. Tall, somber pines marched along the sides of the property; my most profound memories lie in the sound of wind shuttering through their branches. At night, the wind and the moon turned the lake into crinkled tinfoil.

Aside from the house, the grounds featured a boathouse, a dock, and a walkout storage space made of concrete. Above the storage door and facing the lake, a rectangular plaque had been cast with the words "Villa Augusta 1936." In my favorite photo of Grandfather, he's standing in his boat, wearing a suit and tie, Sunday hat pushed back on his head, the habitual cigarette in his mouth. He smiles, lifting one hand in greeting to the photographer. The waters of Lake Hamilton lie dark at his feet, the villa steadfast behind him.

Grandmother always referred to the cottage—living room, bedroom, bath, sleeping porch, and galley kitchen—as her "little, pretty house." Measuring roughly nine hundred square feet, it was made of stucco and patterned after an Italian villa, hence the arches of its front portico. With its floors and cabinetry of knotty pine, however, it had the rustic ambience of a WPA park lodge.

I've arrived in time for supper. Afterward, we settle in the living room. A bricked, wood-burning fireplace, screened for the summer, is the focus of the room. Beside it, Grandfather had fashioned a bookcase with pull-out shelves for his drawing materials, pipe tobacco, and multitudinous copies of the *National Geographic*. Grandmother glances up from her needlework, assessing the bookcase. "You need to thin out those magazines," she says to my grandfather, snipping a thread. "They're taking the place over." Evidently this isn't the first time Granddad has heard this complaint. "I'm not getting rid of any of them," he responds, knocking ashes from his pipe onto a smoking-stand. As if in corroboration, the yellow *Geographics* stand, row after row, their spines military straight. My grandfather waves his pipe in Grandmother's direction. "And when I'm gone, don't you throw them out. They'll be worth something someday." Grandmother says nothing, jabbing her embroidery needle into a hapless pillowcase.

Sitting on the floor beside Granddad's chair, I ask him to please hand me a *Geographic*. The pages of the magazine, polished as glass, invite me into Essex or Tasmania or New Jersey. I'm drawn to a full-page ad for Buick motorcars: A roadster, all curves and seduction, waits gleaming under the question—"Wouldn't you rather have a Buick?" Yes, as it turns out, my grandfather would; he'll soon discard his staid Chevrolet for a Buick, black. In time, my father will do likewise; the Buick indicates discreetly that one has arrived.

The next morning, after breakfast, I hear my grandfather's booming voice. "Come on, Jo Hamel," he says, as I perch on the sofa to buckle my sandals. He uses my middle name, knowing I'm not fond of it. On the second day of my visit, we're departing for the morning's first, solemn chore: feeding the goldfish that live in the midst of Granddad's sumptuous gardens. To make the steeply sloping property navigable, Grandfather created gardens on four levels leading from house to lake. He designed and sculpted the concrete terrace walls and finial urns that mark each set of connecting steps. The goldfish live on the second terrace.

The sun rides my shoulders like a sleeping cat as Granddad and I, fish food in hand, head down the garden steps to the expectant fish. They wait in a small pool featuring a fountain with four sculptured frogs, one for each point of the compass. When I'm not looking, Granddaddy turns a handle at the base of the pool, and water gushes as if by sorcery out of the frogs' mouths. A lizard rattles through the grass.

I measure the fish food according to Granddaddy's instructions. A motorboat, all power and noise, fades in the distance. Far from the hurtling business of the farm, I'm standing in almost unnerving serenity. Grandfather, once the overseer of pumping plants, harrows, and threshing machines, imparts to this moment an even, patient gloss, quiet as the stubbing out of a cigarette.

In one of Mother's art books, I've seen a print of a peasant woman sowing grain in a field. I try to imitate this gesture, casting the fish food evenly upon the water. The goldfish, seeing my outstretched hand, rise up like warriors. Granddad keeps a close eye, frowning if I mete out too much or too little. "Gotta be fair to all the fish," he says. "We can't have any of them mad at us."

Every day, I diligently follow Granddad's instructions. If I'm really good—if I feed the fish just right, if I help my grandmother dust or carry the wash up the basement steps, if I fetch tools for Granddaddy in his shop—maybe God will forgive me for being a cheat. Maybe my parents won't need to argue.

I'm calmed by the order in my grandparents' household. Granddad stores the fish food always on the same shelf. He never loses a sweater. The car keys come to his hand without a search. Unlike my parents' household, where clutter runs amok—eyeglasses and socks held hostage for weeks—the cottage hums through the days unruffled.

Fish-feeding accomplished, Granddad and I stroll back to the house to cool off in front of an Emerson table fan. He looks at his watch; it's time to head to Hot Springs. All the water piped into my grandparents' cottage comes from the lake. It's not fit for human consumption, so Granddad goes into town once a week to buy Mountain Valley spring water. He and Grandmother refuse to drink any other brand. We walk down the moldy stairs from the sleeping porch to the walkout basement, which doubles as a garage. Housing the Chevrolet, a workbench, lawn-mower, and Grandmother's washing machine, the space smells of steel shavings and soap suds. It's cool here; I'd like to stay.

"Hurry up, Slowpoke," Granddad says, faking impatience. "We've got to go." In the car's trunk lie a dozen or so empty, green-tinted glass jugs. They clink as we ease along the gravel road connecting the house to the highway, past a Mom-and-Pop grocery store and a haphazard tourist court. Soon we're on Central Avenue.

Grandfather parks in front of the building housing Mountain Valley's offices—a stunning, white, 1920s Classic Revival. Granddad grumbles, collecting the jugs from the car's trunk, "I bet your grandmother didn't send enough bottles. I should've counted them myself." Once inside, I witness the solemn exchange of old bottles for new. Each one bears the oval red-and-green Mountain Valley logo on which a stream, banked by trees, flows forever toward us, three mountain peaks pristine in the background. I like the logo's ambience, a planet apart from the dust of the farm.

"I guess we won't go thirsty now, Pet," Granddad says, as we step into the car. I settle back in the passenger seat. All's well. We have water for the week, and we'll soon be home for lunch.

———

Some one hundred miles away from the mountains of Hot Springs, under a Delta sky gorging itself on heat, my father stalks through one of his fields, cursing the drought, the shriveled soybeans. Sweat drenches his khaki shirt; it clings to his back like an overgrown barnacle.

"It doesn't look good," he says to my mother at supper. "Don't buy anything you don't have to." He lifts a slice of ham onto his plate. "When's Jo coming home from Hot Springs?"

"In a few days." Mother folds and refolds her napkin. The wall clock, misguided always by forty minutes, ticks on. "She's going to need new school clothes."

"No." My father slams down his fork. "Not until it rains. If it ever rains."

Rain, too much or not enough. Drought, splitting open the dirt of the fields. Grasshoppers and blackbirds, stripping the grain—these are my father's enemies. He pushes back from the table.

If it rains within the week, I'll have new clothes to enter the third grade, and Dad will admire them. If not, I'll hear my parents arguing into the night. It never occurs to either of them, I suppose, to pursue another way of making a living. They are beholden to the spreading sunsets of this forever landscape, to the smells of water irrigating a dry field, to the color of rice at harvest, like burnt butter. They are beholden to the dirt.

———

Granddad wedges the car into the garage. I help him unload the water jugs, storing them on the basement shelves. As Grandfather takes a jug up to the kitchen, I make a mental note to bring the next jug up myself, whenever Grandmother needs it.

Fastening her apron, Grandmother turns to me. "So, *ma cherie*," she says, "what'll we have for lunch?" She knows the answer; it's always the same. "A grilled-cheese sandwich, please." Grandmother produces the Velveeta cheese in its wooden box, the sliced, white Wonder Bread, the Crisco lard, the Hellman's "Real" mayonnaise. She lights a match and turns on the cookstove. With a practiced, whooshing sound the flame settles around the gas ring. Soon the bread is browning, cheese oozing into the grease. These sandwiches, flattened repeatedly by Grandmother's spatula, comprise the main meal—no vegetables, no salad, no fruit. I'm elated. My mother would never countenance such a feast.

Grandmother and I sit alone at the dining-room table, Granddad having gone to Couch's, the nearby marina. The room sags, overcome by a mirrored sideboard, china cabinet, table and six chairs; they seem to be pining for larger quarters. We eat our sandwiches from pink Depression glass plates. For dessert there's cherry pie, another of my favorites. Grandmother, a notoriously careless cook, has made the pie with yellow cherries from which she's forgotten to remove the pits. I proclaim it delicious.

After lunch, Grandmother offers me licorice from the living room's corner cabinet—the one I'm not to open without permission. "They say actresses and singers use licorice," Grandmother observes, taking down a cut-glass bowl with a scalloped rim. "Good for the voice," she says and clicks shut the cabinet door. "When Pappy gets back," she promises, using her pet name for Granddad, "we'll walk down to the store." I don't fancy licorice, but I like the ceremony that comes with it, and I like the way the cabinet's glass doors latch with a bright *ka-krick* that startles the room.

As soon as Grandfather comes through the door, I ask him when he can take me to the marina. I remember from last year its smell of gasoline and boat wax, the display of Chris-Crafts, symbols of speed and wealth. I know my father covets one, and I know my mother will never allow it. Grandmother suggests we head for the store.

"Let me walk the edges," I beg my grandparents, scrambling onto the first of many retaining walls along the graveled route from the cottage to the store. "You'll break your neck," Grandmother predicts. I pay little heed; retaining walls are a novelty in my world. Moss roses and creeping phlox spill over them, giving off a faint odor in the heat. A teacup-size, family-owned endeavor, the grocery smells of cantaloupes. I cajole Grandfather into buying a pint of chocolate ice cream.

———

Almost every day, Granddad took his motorboat out, sprinting around the lake for hours. He seemed happiest when lost in the sound of the motor, speeding under a highway bridge, pointing out to me the grand estates along lake's edge. Grandmother never, to my knowledge, stepped into the boat. She held a dim view of bobbing on open water and kept track of those drowned in Lake Hamilton or nearby Lake Catherine, duly announced in the *Sentinel Record,* the Hot Springs daily.

On one of my visits to my grandparents, when I was twelve or thirteen, a girlfriend invited me to ride in her father's Chris-Craft. I was jubilant—I'd wanted to ride in a Chris-Craft, the Cadillac of speedboats, since I first saw one at the marina. Grandmother, who granted speedboats the same affection she'd give a clutch of black widow spiders, wasn't pleased.

"I don't know about this," she said as I stood ready to leave for my girlfriend's, dressed in my bathing suit. She took hold of my arm. "You be sure to wear a life jacket," she cautioned. "If that boat turns over—listen to me!—nobody's going to think about you. They'll be too busy saving their own daughter." To save face, I protested, but I was taken aback. Though the only one on board to do so, I wore a life jacket, all afternoon.

Despite Grandmother's objections, Grandfather occasionally and with much ado took me out in his boat, to fish. Whether or not we caught anything, I was impressed with Grandfather's knowledge of hidden coves. I trailed one hand in the clanging-cold water, watched trees blur as we passed, noted the outboard motor's consoling smell. Granddad always contrived to get us home just after sunset, a light from the cottage guiding us toward the dock, the dock reassembling itself from the dusk.

Toward evening, in the living room, Granddad and I polish off the chocolate ice cream. The radio's tuned to the nightly news: there's something about the war in Belgium and France. My grandparents, catching a few words of the commentator, exchange a look, a nervous, dark glance, as if a policeman had rapped on the door. I hear words I'm not sure about: "occupation," "deprivation," "enemy lines"—then a word I do know, "starvation." Grandmother begins to fret over her sisters.

From the kitchen, checking her pantry, Grandmother declares she's sending another package of canned goods to Charleroi tomorrow. Grandmother's sisters—"the aunts," as my father referred to them—remained a matter of deep uneasiness in my parents' house, too. To me, these women were immeasurably old and not real; I had never met them. When Grandmother visited Belgium in 1952, she asked me to come along. Charles was becoming my great love, however, and I stayed behind.

I catch the fear in my grandparents' voices. I think of my father's worried face. When I go home, I vow silently, I'll refill Dad's iced-tea glass as often as he wants. Without grumbling.

At Grandmother's death, the cottage and grounds passed to my father. He replaced Granddad's boat with one that was sleeker and louder, purchased at Couch's. He used it to teach my husband, me, and our children to water ski on Lake Hamilton. Villa Augusta became the family getaway.

When I inherited the property in 2000, it had lain neglected for at least seven years. I wondered how I could afford to keep it. A target for squatters and vandals, the cottage needed gargantuan repairs. The boat-house had rotted, and the wooden pier was gone, along with grandfather's fountain frogs, smashed by delinquents. Stragglers had littered the now overgrown and slovenly terraces: a pair of one-legged sunglasses here, a rain-soaked Gideon Bible there, a red, high-heeled shoe. Wherever I walked, I could hear my grandfather's generous laugh and my grandmother's call to supper. The wind in the giant pines hummed just as I remembered—remote, circumspect, hinting at remorse.

I brought my daughter to her great-grandmother's cottage one fall day in 1995 or 1996. Charla was stunned by its emptiness, surprised by how much smaller the rooms were than she remembered. She talked about her good times here in the late 1960s and early 1970s: swimming, water skiing, eating Mother's picnic lunches—German potato salad always included—on the dock. She had teased her great-granddad about a garbled-together series of ropes and pulleys that he'd built to transport himself up the steep rise from lake to house, avoiding the wearisome steps.

Charla also remembered the piles of ancient magazines throughout the house, dating from my grandmother's reign. "I used to cut them up for school reports—the pictures and stuff," she confided. "I was always afraid Granddaddy would find out." She recalled sunbathing on the dock with Aunt Nancy and their hours of drifting, companionable talk.

I think of my sister as she was then, in her teens and early twenties, with a delightful sense of humor and a penchant for playing practical jokes on Dad. Her resemblance to Daddy and Grandmother Garot is striking—part of the reason, perhaps, that Dad called on Nancy, not me, for help with the outboard or a repair in the boathouse or a quick trip to the marina. As Nancy distanced herself from Mother, I speculate, the bonds between my sister and Dad tightened. I wasn't aware then or later of sibling rivalry, although one of Nancy's lawyers attempted to make that case. Before the court appearance in which I appealed to have Nancy and me removed as co-executrices, her lawyer wrote in his brief that my action was based on "jealousy, greed, and remorse." In his brief, my attorney retorted, "Self-serving muck."

Of course I wonder—before two people come to the impasse of courtrooms and lawyers, while they think themselves friends—what precipitates the first, almost imperceptible fault in the relationship? Before and during the settling of the estate, my sister pointedly distanced herself from me, with the resulting emotional and financial trauma—at least for me. It may be, I conclude, that although layers of issues interweave in its dynamics, a family's destiny rests in the basic equation of who resembles—and acts like—whom.

As Charla and I entered the cottage, long emptied of its worn Art Deco furniture and clutter of *Geographics,* a scene from a summer evening I'd spent there rose in my mind: *We're finished with supper. Granddad is reading, lighting and relighting his pipe. Grandmother tells her husband of the day's news—a neighbor's visit, a tiff over who will host the church supper next week, a cousin down with the flu. Grandfather listens and nods, then reads something from the evening paper to Grandmother. My grandparents seem to delight in these small events, forgetting the murmuring radio, tuning out the meddlesome world.*

Thinking me asleep on the sofa, my grandparents converse in French. I lie still under the rise and fall of their voices, the fluid collisions of words I don't need to understand.

———

The legendary romance of my paternal grandparents is to our family history as a bird-of-paradise to the Sahara. Although both lived in Charleroi, my future grandparents scarcely knew each other: when Pierre departed for America, he was eleven and Augusta two. Augusta grew up into a winsome young woman; my grandfather, returning to his hometown intermittently over the course of eighteen years, took notice. Back in the States after one of his visits, he sent for Augusta to come to New Orleans to be his bride. According to my father, Mamá and Papá Fenasse were not amused. They thought Pierre too old for their daughter, by nine years. Moreover, she would be going to America; it might as well have been Tasmania. They vowed to disinherit her if she married "that man."

Augusta hied herself to Antwerp and boarded a ship bound for New Orleans.

The rift between my grandmother and her parents endured, my father always said, until he was ten. Then Augusta's parents, wanting to see their grandson, relented, and Dad sailed with his mother and father to Charleroi. "My grandmother Fenasse was mean," Dad remembered. "She rapped my knuckles with her dressmaking yardstick when I tracked mud into the house."

That's the story of my grandparents' courtship and marriage—Dad's version. Charles and I visited Charleroi in 2005, having located Augusta's niece Antoinette, then in her eighties. When Grandmother left Charleroi, Antoinette was too young to remember, but she had heard the stories of her aunt Augusta. I asked Antoinette if what I had heard from my father was valid.

"No!" Antoinette exclaimed, amused, speaking through an interpreter. "That's not the way it was at all. Your grandmother's parents were happy she'd found someone who could support her!" I was dismayed to learn that the story I'd heard all my life, the one in which my belligerent and romantic grandmother glitters like mica, may not be true.

Whichever story more closely fits the truth, my grandmother Garot clearly possessed grit, a quality she would need as a pioneer rice farmer's wife. Before leaving Charleroi, I visited the house Grandmother grew up in. I imagined her standing in the doorway with her suitcases, dressed in a saucy hat for her journey, not sure she'd ever see this house again.

I consulted with Antoinette about another family legend: Grandmother's youngest sister, Emilia, according to Dad, served in the French resistance during World War I, in German-occupied Belgium. Antoinette confirmed the story, verifying as well that Emilia had been captured by the Germans and confined in prison. Her country later awarded her the Croix de Guerre.

———

When Grandfather Garot died, I was twelve; Nancy was a toddler. Although the practice of having a wake at home was by then already out of fashion, Dad insisted that his father lie in state in the dining room of the farmhouse. Grandmother sat there for two days and nights, holding her husband's hand. I wandered the house, bewildered by this turn of events—my grandmother's withdrawal from my sister and me, the somber bustle in the rooms, my father's tears.

In his day, Granddad caused this corner of the Delta to make way for his house and farm. He claimed this dirt, then left it for a time. Finally, he has returned.

———

Grandmother outlived Granddad by ten years, staying on at the lake, keeping up the house and grounds. Having never learned to drive, she relied on friends to take her shopping and to church. I'm sure her early years as a widow were filled with doubt. In a stenographer's notebook I found in her effects, Grandmother had written herself step-by-step instructions for performing unaccustomed chores: lighting the floor furnace, adjusting the hot-water heater, switching to lake water, and draining the cistern. As I held the notebook, Grandmother's frustration and grief bristled in my hand. I thought of the day when such bewilderment may come to me.

Eventually, with almost debilitating regret, I sold the villa, salvaging the plaque with Grandmother's name, the parts of my grandfather's bookcase that reside in my study now, and a wooden oar: talismans of a fabled time and my place in it.

My grandparents Garot visited the farm sporadically in their retirement, usually at planting time, when the dirt smells powerful and clean. They occupied the guest bedroom, which looks to the neighboring land of Alex Lepine, far from the Louisiana disasters. As a child, I would often find my grandmother in that upstairs room, reading her Bible. One Easter—I was nine or ten—she gave me a specially treated plaque inscribed "The Lord is my shepherd. . . ." I put it beside my bed. That night, and for countless nights to come, it glowed in the dark.

CHAPTER 11

City

In those nonchalant summers of my childhood, when I scampered off the farm to visit relatives in Hot Springs or Cabot or North Little Rock, I discovered another layer of being beyond my father's fields. I was beginning to internalize the contrasts of other landscapes and cultures to our Delta farm, beginning to understand who I was. The lakes, the mountains, the Arlington Hotel of Hot Springs, the rises and swales of Grandfather Merritt's rocky farm—those momentarily seduced me, but, although I had no words for it then, the dirt of the land I grew up on had seeped into my bones.

Little Rock, the largest city in Arkansas then and now, lies just across the Arkansas River from North Little Rock, where my cousins Mollie and Albert lived in a circumspect red-brick house at 2019 North Main. Childless, they welcomed me into their house for a week each summer, usually at the end of my stay with my grandparents Merritt, who lived less than an hour's drive away.

The two cities provided a sharp contrast to the farm and rural southeast Arkansas. In the relatively urban world of Mollie and Albert, the land lay in precise city blocks, more than one movie house existed, and there were no mosquitoes. That world, however, lacked the luxurious dirt of my backyard. It lacked even the dirt sufficient for mud pies, a fact I lament in a letter home during one of my visits. I'm not yet nine at the writing of this letter, dated June 6, 1944, D-Day: the Allied invasion of Normandy against the Germans in World War II. I remained unaware of this, and I don't recall any mention of that historic event in my cousins' house.

June 6, 1944

Dear daddy and mother,

How are things at home?

Please don't throw away my mud pies. I want them to play with when I come home.

We are going to the zoo this afternoon. Yesterday evening we went to the airport to watch the planes come in.

Albert has decided we are going to have a weinie roast. I found a four leaf clover yesterday. . . . We fed the birds this morning but it was only the sparrows that got it.

Tomorrow we are going to the house where McAurther was born.

I hope you didn't sell my bicycle and tent daddy.

There isn't any dust up here to make mud pies.

Lots of love,

Jo

Even though the deep dust of the farm found no purchase in my cousins' city, every day of my visits there held some fillip of delight. Albert, older than Mollie by over a decade and semi-retired from his furniture business, took me occasionally to the movies. (In a letter written on one of my visits, I tell Daddy that I've seen Lou Costello, one of Dad's favorites, in *Who Done It?*) Mollie, Albert, and I went to Lakewood to see the Old Mill, which, as most Arkansans know, made a cameo appearance in the movie *Gone with the Wind*. We went to Burns Park, the largest park I had ever seen, its woods going on and on, green and cool and mysterious. I had read about Robin Hood, and I imagined him in a forest like this. We crossed the river into Little Rock, down Main to Little Rock's air-conditioned stores, the ones with mannequins wearing winter coats in mid-July. At Pfeiffer's, the icy temperature made me long for one of those coats. I rode the elevators aimlessly while Mollie bought a girdle and a pair of stockings.

Part of the joy of visiting Mollie and Albert lay in showing off, using my best penmanship and sentence structure, in letters home to my parents. Dad, chronically worried about my drooping math skills, would surely have been pleased by my account, written on a visit when I was eight, of buying a comic book in Little Rock. "Today," I write, "I got a funny-book. I forgot my purse and told Mollie. She payed for it. I didn't ask her to but she did. I payed her back with two nickels because it was a dime."

In my cousins' house, I fell into the rhythm of their days. The day would begin with a breakfast of bacon, eggs fried over-easy, sausage, and orange juice. Mollie and I would wash the dishes, stacking them in a red plastic rack beside the sink to dry. Albert might go to the furniture store for a few hours or putter in the yard.

One particular visit, when I was ten, stands illuminated in my memory. On the second day of my visit, a Monday, after breakfast and the washing-up, Mollie and I retreated to the master bedroom, where I was allowed to watch as she solemnly pinned up her mass of waist-length hair. I sat on the edge of the four-poster bed; Mollie settled herself in front of an Art Deco vanity with a huge round mirror, tinted blue at its edges. It was understood we would not speak during this ritual; Mollie's utmost concentration was required as, bobby pins in her mouth, she brushed, braided and fastened, brushed, braided and fastened. I'd never seen such long, thick hair on a young person, much less someone I considered old. (At the time of this visit, Mollie was probably in her early fifties.)

I wanted to run my fingers through these strands before Mollie captured them in braids, but I didn't dare ask. The only sounds in the room were the brush repeating itself again and again through my cousin's chestnut-brown, graying hair. Next came the dust-mopping under the family-room cot, finding Albert's stray house slippers, which Mollie referred to as "dogs": "We're barking the dogs out," she'd joke. Bed pillows lolled on the cot for Albert's midday nap, and Mollie tucked in the pillowslips' open sleeves to "keep the bugs and critters out." When I made my bed in the front room allotted me for my visit, I followed Mollie's example with the pillowcases, though I never mastered her precise tucks and folds.

Being Monday, this was wash day. Mollie and I retreated to the laundry room, adjacent to the garage, where I helped her sort the clothes, colors apart from white, before the Maytag took them. (All the womenfolk in our family favored Maytags.) I was happy to do this; I'd become something of an expert at it, helping Mother. Besides, the concrete-floored laundry room, thick roofed and under the shade of a pecan tree, remained cool all day, and almost any chore was worth doing that kept us out of the lunging heat.

Mary was waiting in the laundry room. An elderly black woman,

Mary came three days a week to help Mollie with the washing, ironing, or housework. I knew her from my previous visits, and I liked to be in her ample presence.

As Mollie had never learned to drive, it was Albert's job to fetch Mary early on the mornings she came to the Andrews—I've no idea from where. Albert told me Mary didn't know how old she was and that she couldn't read or write. In my ten-year-old exuberance, I resolved to teach Mary, on the days she came to Mollie's, to write her name. Thus began my teaching career.

Mary sat in her usual spot, on a bench at one wall, her back poker straight, hands folded, waiting for Mollie's orders. I went back into the house, begged a small, lined notebook and a #2 pencil from Albert. "Let's learn to write your name," I chirped to Mary, returning to the laundry room. Mollie's mouth fell open in surprise. Panic took over Mary's usually placid face. She fiddled with a strand of frizzled gray hair, clasped and unclasped her hands, adjusted the belt around her ample waist. Sparrows scritch-scratched in the gutters. A train sounded in the distance. Finally, Mary announced, "I can't, Miss Jo." Glancing at Mollie, she said, "You know I have to help Miss Mollie with the clothes. No'm. I can't."

Undaunted, I asked Mollie if she could spare Mary for a little while each day that she came to work, explaining my mission. Mollie agreed; we could start that very afternoon, after Mary had finished the ironing. Thus the pact was made—much, I imagine, to Mary's chagrin.

From the start of our first lesson, Mary was perspiring, holding the pencil tightly enough to break it, biting her bottom lip, frowning. After fifteen minutes or so, she stood and announced, "Please tell Mr. Albert I'm ready to go home," gathering up her elephantine handbag and the leftover chicken backs Mollie had given her.

I was relentless in my efforts to promote Mary from illiteracy, ready, each morning that she came to Mollie's, with a clean sheet of paper and a freshly sharpened pencil. I made the laundry room my classroom for a week, garnering time with Mary in the mornings and afternoons. I don't remember how many hours Mary endured there, amidst the smells of starch and Oxydol, but on "graduation" day, just before I left for home, Mary produced, in wavering, thin strokes, the letters of her name.

I was disappointed that my first pupil gave me nary a smile or a thank you. In my hubris, I had assumed everyone wanted to learn to write his or her name. Later I came to understand that Mary's reluctance stemmed from embarrassment. Indeed, it was I who had been taught: Mary gave me a lesson in empathy, one I've tried, not always successfully, to carry into my classrooms.

———

Even on wash days, Mollie produced lunch at the stroke of noon. Fried chicken was her masterpiece. The chicken pieces were soaked in milk, dredged in flour, dropped in popping-hot lard, then cooked until tender over a moderate flame. Despite the sputtering grease, Mollie kept the gas range spit-polish clean. Her kitchen was spacious, filled with plants and whatnots. I was particularly taken with a green ceramic match safe nailed to the wall beside the stove. (It's in my kitchen today.) Mollie's collection of outsized salt and pepper shakers stood at attention on a shelf above it.

Range hoods and vent fans hadn't yet come into popular use in the early 1940s; Mollie would simply turn the oscillating pedestal fan to a higher speed, shooing the cooking steam and odors through the open windows, and we'd sit down to eat.

In the afternoons of my visits, I would walk around the block, sometimes twice; Mollie insisted I get exercise. Purplish, huge boils plagued me every summer, and Mollie and Grandmother Merritt made it their joint project to cure me; vigorous walking was one of their remedies. It didn't help, but I liked the neatly painted houses on the block, the heavy odor of gardenias, the brisk, purposeful traffic, and—most of all—the talk that drifted from porches.

Mollie and Albert had next-door neighbors, a novelty to me; our nearest neighbor at home was across a field. Mrs. Lattimer lived in a house so close to Mollie's that sunlight could barely wriggle between them. The house culminated in a latticed back porch we could see from Mollie's family room. Once in a while Mrs. Lattimer's voice shimmered from the porch through our open windows, and Mollie would suggest, "Let's go over and say hello. I believe she's receiving." Although I'm sure we visited, I don't remember ever seeing the neighbor; she remains a voice behind a lattice on a summer day.

My cousins' social life revolved around informal gatherings on porches and weekly visits from Granddaddy Merritt, who stopped by with sacks of snap beans or crowder peas from Grandmother's garden. This was occasion to gather round the kitchen table and devour slices of Mollie's three-layer coconut cake, for which she was famous. The talk grazed the same subjects on every visit: Grandmother's garden, the weather, Granddad's corn crop, my progress in school, and Uncle Coy's latest illness or marital woe. Curiously, although the *Arkansas Gazette* and the radio carried daily news of the war raging in Europe, it was never mentioned at that table.

The family room, also called the sunroom, faced onto a neatly trimmed backyard. A small maple tapped its leaves now and again against one of the sunroom's windows, as if wanting to engage us in conversation. The room was light filled, haphazard, and cozy. Albert kept stacks of *Field and Stream* magazines on a corner bookshelf; one afternoon, when Mollie deemed it too hot for me to walk, I prowled through them. Inadvertently, I turned to an article about an Indian village plagued nightly by a man-eating tiger. Mesmerized, transported across continents to that village, I saw the tiger creep toward a sleeping boy and lunge. I smelled the tiger's breath; the boy's screams filled my own throat. Outside, a robin or a finch might have been singing, but I heard nothing, in another country, dumb and deaf with terror.

———

The house at 2019 North Main lives in my memory like a beloved character of a novel. The sun never invaded as it did at home; it entered hesitantly through venetian blinds only when invited. Because of Albert's business, the furniture in the house was of excellent quality, mostly mahogany—except in the sunroom, a hodgepodge of skewed lamps, crooked end tables, chairs of dubious ancestry, and Albert's cot.

I memorized everything in those rooms: the painting in the dining room, a still-life with a copper pan and grapes. The marble-topped library table in the living room with three books held in place by ceramic bookends: a boy in orange shorts and a girl in a polka-dot skirt, both with open books on their laps. The Lucite comb and brush set on Mollie's vanity. A ceramic cat, a calico, curled on the hearth of the formal living room's fireplace, which, even at Christmas, was never used. The living-room draperies hung in maroon-velvet serenity, and the area rugs were springy and thick. Mollie's mother, my aunt Alice, had lain in her casket in this room; Mollie said it made her sad to enter it, so she kept its French doors closed.

I made the living room my sanctuary, bringing a book there every afternoon, arranging myself on the stern mohair sofa to read. Under the glow of a reproduction-Tiffany lamp on the library table, my anxiety over grades and school and my parents' arguments left me. Those afternoons, I became some other self—the beholder of Black Beauty, maybe the girl of the Limberlost.

I could count on at least two hours, most days, to lose myself in a book. Although he approved of my bookworm leanings, Albert would interrupt me every afternoon around four o'clock. "Let's have a snack," he'd say, leading me into the kitchen where he produced the ice cream sandwiches we both adored: two thin chocolate wafers and one small scoop of Yarnell's vanilla ice cream, assembled on Mollie's spotless tile counter. To this day I crave those sandwiches, and updated kitchens with granite counters and stainless-steel appliances don't hold the charm, for me, of an all-white kitchen, its side door opening onto a yard with two trees.

—————

I believe I derived whatever sense of humor I may have from Albert. In my parents' house, the tone was mostly urgent and resolute. A living had to be made in a precarious, fickle business. Although my father had a ready, dry wit, it was Albert, with his practical jokes and banter and well-meant teasing, who taught me to take myself less seriously, who taught me how to laugh.

Albert loved playing the rascal. His favorite targets were my mother and one of Granddad Merritt's nieces, Tera. In a 1933 letter written to Mother at the university, Tera, a house guest in the Merritt household, relates the highlights of a Sunday visit paid by Mollie and Albert.

> May 20, 1933
> Jacksonville, Arkansas
>
> Dear Ruth,
>   Mollie and Albert came by Sunday. We had a good dinner, of course—squirrel and ice cream and cake. . . . Albert had to have

his joke—while out picking lettuce Sunday, he picked up a toad, wrapped it in lettuce and paper, and brought it in the house and put it on my lap. Of course the paper fell off and there was a frog. I screamed and Albert got a good laugh. Can't you just hear him. He wants me to bring the frog home with me. He's still in the yard, the toad I mean.

Love, Tera

Mollie and Albert's world engaged my imagination partly because it had nothing to do with farming. Mollie had been raised on my grandfather Merritt's acreage, but happily adapted to life in the city. Sitting on Mollie's front porch felt nothing like sitting on Grandmother Merritt's. Cars slushed constantly by. The melding sound of crickets and evening birds in Mollie's yard was doused by traffic, disappearing like a chiffon handkerchief tossed onto water. Occasionally a neighbor across the street brought over honey from hives on his property—a Mr. Madden, I think, who stayed for iced tea and lemon cookies. Mollie served the tea in tall glasses stamped with red and yellow poppies. Nestled in their vintage caddy, the glasses rattled amiably on their way to the porch.

Its population only twenty-one thousand or so in 1940, North Little Rock nevertheless gave me a sense of city life. I liked the order of my cousins' household, where schedules were predictable, not contingent upon the weather or harvest or the breakdowns of machinery. Here, supper was at an appointed time. No one dressed in khakis, and the evening yard filled with fireflies, never mosquitoes. I was a child of the farm at heart, but urban life was a welcome respite.

———

Although my time with Mollie and Albert was mostly sunny, I learned some dark life lessons in their company. Most pervasive was the melancholy I sensed in Mollie. From the time I first remember her, Mollie wore cotton house dresses, all cut from the same pattern: wide-collared, buttoned to the waist, and belted. They lay flat from the neck down; in childish curiosity and naïveté, I asked Mollie why her dresses fit that way. "Cancer," she explained, her mouth turning downward. "They had to take my bosoms." I wasn't sure, at five, what "bosoms" meant, but I didn't ask, and Mollie quickly changed the subject. She had developed a habit of smoothing the tops of her dresses over her absent breasts, as if still expecting them there—frowning, flicking her hands down her shirtwaist as if dismissing a fly.

My own loss, the first one I remember, occurred on a vacation taken with Mollie and Albert when I was five, in December of 1940. They had joined Mother, Dad, and me in Pensacola, Florida, for a few days. We were there in winter because it was the only season my father could leave the farm. On the first day of vacation, Albert and I walked the ocean's edge looking for seashells. Albert was dressed as if going to his store, in a three-piece suit and fedora hat, a gold watch chain across his vest. I wore a misshapen wool coat my mother had made from one of hers.

"That's a good-looking bucket, Missy," Albert said, nodding toward the sand bucket, complete with spade, that my father had bought me when we arrived in town. Electric-blue waves cavorted on its yellow background, and its handle was lipstick red. I squatted in the sand, mindful of my Sunday coat, about to scoop sand into the bucket, holding it by the bail. I daydreamed, picturing this prize, this symbol of all things colorful and fun in the world, in my sandbox at home. I felt a sudden pull on the bucket, and it was gone, swallowed like Jonah in the whale.

Devastated, outraged, I turned to Albert. "My bucket! Get it! You've got to get it! Please!" Albert shook his head. "It's gone, Honey. The ocean's got it now." I was stunned. The bucket was brand-new; I hadn't even really played with it yet. How could it be lost? But lost it was, to the wave, exacting and impersonal, that had taken it out of my hand.

"Right out of my hand," I sniveled later to my father. "What did you expect?" he grumbled, irritated that his investment had been swept out to the Gulf of Mexico. "You should have known better." Albert should have stopped me, my father said; he should have been watching.

On my studio bookshelf there's a photo of me on that beach, holding Albert's hand in one hand, the sand bucket in the other. Albert and I smile, squinting in the sunlight. Columns of seacoast clouds laze plump and overfed above the ocean. Someone has snapped us in the moment before disaster.

⸻

During a summer visit with Mollie and Albert when I was eleven or twelve, we spent a few days in Eureka Springs, Arkansas's postcard picturesque town. It's a stair-step village in the Ozarks, rickracking its way up the hills, providing such attractions as a hotel whose upper story one enters from the street. Albert secured a tourist cabin on Lake Leatherwood, a lake he deemed good for fishing. The rock cabin was small and dark but offered a kitchenette where Mollie could fry the fish we'd catch.

I fell in love with a town that summer. Eureka Springs had earned its name, reportedly, from the "Eureka!" moment when a doctor discovered its healing waters. It attracted artists, poets, musicians, craftsmen, and bums and offered the tacky and the exotic in its shops. For my cousins and me, it supplied an escape from Little Rock's wilting humidity and heat. I was allowed to wander the terrain near Lake Leatherwood. In a dry creek bed near the lake, I found a flattened serving spoon that inexplicably seemed a treasure. It's tucked away in my cutlery drawer; I smile every time I see it.

My time in Eureka would have been idyllic—fishing, eating the fish with Mollie's corn on the cob and hash browns, walking the town's steep, complicated streets—except for my boils. The polio season was upon us, and Mollie was sure that lake water in combination with boils would spell disaster. She was adamant that I not swim in Lake Leatherwood, even though I promised to cover every boil with a Band-Aid.

———

The wonder of the past, it seems to me, is not that so much is forgotten but that so much survives—and is indelible, at least for a time. Nearly seventy years have passed since my walk with Albert on that Florida beach, but I remember perfectly the cold, the ocean's dark smell, the broken white shells on the white beach, my hand in Albert's hand.

Nothing tangible remains of those days with Mollie and Albert except Kodak snapshots, one bookend, the mountain-with-stream painting, and the ceramic cat, which I inherited at Mollie's death. The house on North Main is gone, along with Mrs. Lattimer's, whisked into a church parking lot. The memories, of course, stay, visited and revisited—so much so that the familiar threatens to become unfamiliar. Mollie and Albert and all my lost relatives, once dear and uncomplicated in my mind, now under scrutiny dance away from me—living their lives, near strangers.

———

In a snapshot taken on the farm, Mother and Dad, Mollie and Albert, Grandfather Merritt, and I are in a field of harvest-ready oats. I assume Grandmother Merritt is in the field, too, taking the photo. It's late August 1939; I'll be four in December. Mother carries me, for the oats are far taller than I am, almost to my father's shoulders. Why have we gathered here? I think Dad's farming operation, so different from their worlds, held a particular fascination for my mother's cousins and her parents. Probably they've asked my father for a tour.

Perhaps in this moment that the snapshot captures, these folk who loved me and loved my parents are congratulating my father on his crop, predicting a generous harvest. My father, grandfather, and Albert, all in hats, are smiling, standing behind me and my mother, their faces just visible above the sralks. In a few days, on September 1, Germany will invade Poland. Distanced from the rattle of war to come, this little band stands secure, surrounded by a farm's bounty and the coppery, blunt smell of maturing grain, oblivious to the coming dark.

CHAPTER 12

A Circle in the Ground

SHE REMEMBERS A HOUSE

After school,
stepping down from the bus,
walking between my father's fields,
past the hollyhocks
my mother forgets to water,
skirting my sister's bike,
I enter that house,
all our galoshes pell mell on the porch.

It's a warm, silky day in January 1995, a Saturday. Taking a break from teaching to visit Arkansas, I've asked my grandchildren to come with me to the homeplace. I want to show them the imaginary circle in the ground—the house, the barn, the fields—where I grew up. I want to tell them my story.

Besides my grandchildren and me, our group includes Charla, Chris, and Cindy, my then daughter-in-law. Duke hasn't come along. A few miles west of DeWitt, we turn off the highway onto a county road—paved now, squelching the dust my mother so despised. The house comes into view, sitting on a slight rise, surrounded by fields. We turn onto the long, sweeping lane that leads to the house. "It's like being in another time," comments one of my granddaughters, "like way back when." We persuade the wilting iron gate, remaindered from my paternal grandparents, to let us into the yard. I note the peeling paint of the house and the patchy grass in the yard, although our cousin Emile Lepine, Alex Lepine's grandson, graciously keeps it mowed. Emile and his brother, Edwin, rent the homeplace land; thus the farming operation continues in Dad's absence. No one has lived on the place for over five years, and it's been longer than that since I've seen it.

Stunned by the grimness of the place, I stand with my family on the lawn, looking at brambles and small trees where Mother's garden plot had been. "It's like an enchanted garden," Cindy says, "just like in the movie." Pecans from trees planted in Grandfather Garot's time litter the ground. We drift closer to the garden. The rickety plank crossing the drainage ditch still stands, as well as the wire fence where, over fifty years ago, I was traumatized by a simple garden spider in its web.

I'm distracted by the past wavering before me. Nearby sits the metal swing set and slide—decorated now with flowerets of rust—that Mother and Dad installed for my sister's fifth birthday. I see Nancy as she was that April day, dressed for her party in a gray organdy dress, flying down the slide.

Beside the swing set, Dad had planted a miniature windmill he'd bought on a whim. Mother had viewed it as "double ugly" and an insult to the yard. My daughter remembers it from childhood visits. It pitches to one side now and bears a coat of rust, but the blades still turn. "Look," Charla says with delight, "it still works. I've got to tell Duke."

Weakened by treatments for the cancer that will take her life in four years, Charla's sitting beside the swing set on an overturned bucket that Chris finds in the wash shed. Chris knew my parents well, having farmed with Daddy for a time. He and Charla and their oldest child, Tanner, reminisce about my folks and that time on the farm. Tanner, nearly sixteen, was seven when my mother died; he remembers her, the windmill, a Christmas supper or two in the farmhouse, one of Mother's long-dead cats. His brother, Chandler, is twelve; his twin sisters, Shea and Lauren, are fourteen. Although they don't remember Mother, they share recollections of Dad in his last years—his hugs, his continuing love of Creole gumbo, the "awful" felt hat he wore year-round. Duke and Cindy's son Collin, eight, remembers Dad vaguely; his brother, Merritt, five, remembers neither of my parents.

Time has pillaged and raped; my old homeplace looks like the setting for a Tennessee Williams play: genteel decay in the Old South. It's no wonder Daddy, after Mother's death, discouraged my coming here, insisting we meet elsewhere. It's evident he kept nothing up in the house or yard after Mother died. Perhaps he simply stopped caring. There's a constant ache in my throat, seeing on one hand the graying place that neglect has claimed, and on the other the shimmering vista of earlier days.

Despite the Gothic gloom, I see that this visit is important to my daughter. She'd spent many summer days here, rattling into town in the pickup with her grandfather, aggravating her grandmother in the kitchen, wandering the dust-heaped roads.

Four years Duke's senior, Charla is the oldest link, other than me and my sister, in the chain of memory connecting me to my parents. Her death will break that chain. Fiercely family oriented, Charla remembers her grandparents with affection and candor. "Those atrocious plastic boots of Granddaddy's!" she'd often exclaim to me, laughing. "Can't you make him get rid of them?" Then she'd add, "Bless his heart." Many stories about my parents will disappear with Charla, stories only she can remember.

"Let's go out to the lot," I suggest. "We'll come back to the house later." We make our way to the quadrangle, once the hub of the farm, outlined by my father's shop, a garage for the farm trucks, various sheds, the grain dryer, the barn, and the watering trough for the lone horse.

My grandsons stand in awe before the 1930s gasoline pump on the edge of the lot. A service-station model, eight feet tall, the pump—technically known as a dispenser—was manually operated and relied on gravity. Gas was pumped from an underground tank into a tall, clear glass cylinder, the cylinder culminating in a globe etched with the logo of Standard Oil. Gallon markers documented the gasoline's climb to the globe, where it collected before murmuring slowly down, delivered by hose and nozzle into some waiting car or truck. As a teenager finally allowed to drive, I took inordinate pleasure in gassing up the pickup for my escapes to town, the coveted odor of gasoline alive on my hands.

Duke has often told me how, as a child, he watched spellbound as his grandfather pumped the gasoline "clear to the top," as the gas, pale pink in color, sloshed and rattled the steel markers on its way.

We move on to Dad's shop, my favorite spot as a child. My stomach knots. Was it always this ugly, this small? Its primitive wooden door sticks as it always did, determined against strangers. I walk along the scarred wood counter, touching things: the grease-soaked toolbox, the wrenches, the vise. I'm remembering Dad solemn in this workplace, in a rush to make repairs, to get back in the field. A tractor or plow or combine would be sagging, waiting its turn for parts, on the concrete apron.

The small, potbellied woodstove, never adequate for heating the place, stands in the corner it always claimed, the bellows hanging above it. I see my father, fanning and cursing a sluggish winter fire, and Bill, blowing on his hands to warm them, waiting for orders.

I smile, seeing under the work counter my red wagon, rusted now and lopsided, holding memories of summer, Bill, and our careening rides.

Slowly, we continue our circuit of the farm's outbuildings. In one of them, Tanner and Chandler gleefully discover my father's 1961 Chevrolet Apache 10 pickup. Later this year, on his sixteenth birthday and to his jubilation, the truck will become Tanner's. This would have pleased my father. Having kept every vehicle he ever owned, he'd have seen, in this case, his hoarding justified.

I tell the group I'd like to explore the pumping-plant shed; it sits not far from the shop. Chris suggests we stay put while he goes ahead, scouting the boisterous weeds for snakes. "Mom," he says, returning, "are you sure you want to go out there? The shed's in really bad shape. It's falling in, and it's filthy." Curiosity and nostalgia propel me; I have to see it. Collin, Tanner, and Cindy come along, but the rest of the group fan out on forays of their own.

I step into the one-room shed that housed, in my memory, first Virgil, then Bob, in the mosquito-riddled summers they spent here, nursing the Fairbanks engine. "How did anyone live this way," I think, shocked at the poverty of the room. As a child, when I visited Virgil's wife, Loretta, in these quarters, I thought little of the lack of plumbing or a cookstove, or of the heat, easily ten degrees above the grueling temperature outside. I tell my small audience about the ease with which Loretta occupied these dingy quarters, treating me as if I were a grown-up come to tea. "She couldn't have been over eighteen," I say, "but she was the epitome of grace." Tanner and Cindy want to know what happened to her. "After one season of the heat and mosquitoes," I answer, "she and Virgil went up North to work in the factories. I never saw them again."

Replacing Loretta's cheerful feed-sack curtain, a gunnysack hangs over the shed's one window. Rotting boards, great piles of Dad's ubiquitous paper sacks, and a rodent-eaten mattress add to the squalor. Collin frowns, touching my arm. "Your Dad—he never threw out anything, did he? Why?" Chris looks at me and smiles, having been witness to Dad's eccentric ways. I tell Collin I wish I had an answer.

In the building adjoining the shack, the imperious Fairbanks still towers. Long unused, it's soon to be shuttled to the oil fields of Texas or Oklahoma or sold for scrap. I'm sixty years old on this visit, but seeing this skulking monster I'm a child, tagging along with my father as he conducts a routine engine check. Dad's voice is no-nonsense: I'm not to go near the Fairbanks or the almost-endless, unstable belt it powers. A familiar fear rises in my mouth, a taste like old metal.

Bob, successor to Virgil in the pumping shed, was a wiry, indomitable man who endured my father's anger and churlish pay for some fifty years. Rough edged and outspoken, with many personal tics, Bob was probably a misfit everywhere except on this farm, nursing the Fairbanks, walking levees, milking, driving a tractor—doing the bidding of my father.

Bob had an ear for gossip, and the impasse between me and Nancy over the estate was well circulated in DeWitt. When Bob heard of it, he remarked, so I was told, that he wasn't surprised. "They was spoiled, them girls," he reportedly said. "Their mother, now, Miss Ruth—there was a sweetheart." After Dad died, Bob was heard to comment that my father was "mean and stingy," adding, "I loved that old man, though, bless his flint heart." Until I heard of those remarks, I hadn't considered the love-hate bond that must have existed between my father and Bob, forged of resentment, grudging respect, and practical need.

Sobered by the abysmal sight of the pumping shed, our small group joins the rest of the clan to proceed to the barn. As we pass by broken, scattered equipment, Merritt shakes his head with the gravity of a five-year-old. "This stuff looks *bad*," he declares. I tell him some of it dates back to his great-great-grandfather Garot's time.

We reach the barn, the visual centerpiece of the farm, built of native cypress planks—unavailable these days due to overlogging—that had aged to a silvery gray. Our spirits lift. Years later, when I ask my grandchildren what impressed them most about this visit, the barn wins, hands down. The smell of dank, abandoned hay greets us; sunlight worms its way through chinks in the cypress boards. I help my grandchildren scramble up the makeshift ladder to see the view from the loft. I describe the horse and the unpleasant milk cow who once occupied these stanchions. We discover two Victorian-era black buggies huddled in a corner.

I wonder to myself where these buggies came from. Did Mother buy them for a customer? How did she transport them here? My father had declared when she opened the shop that if Mother bought any furniture or "anything that has to go in a truck," he wasn't about to haul it. Was there a quarrel? Or had Dad himself secretly bought the buggies and hidden them from Mother's view, as he'd done when he purchased the Lincoln? I think of those buggies now and then, the surprise of them, dark in a dark corner of the barn—keeping their secrets, wise as pharaohs.

I've discovered much about my parents' past lives, but the paradox persists: the closer I get, the farther they flee. My father, who prided himself on being enigmatic, would have loved this admission.

We proceed to a building on the edge of the old threshing lot. Missing its sliding doors, it shelters assorted junk and two grain carts. Tanner clambers up to peer into one and reports a long-dead, fraying squirrel. I imagine the hunger for grain that led the squirrel down the slick, inside precipice of the metal cart, then the clawing up and falling back, again, again, again, desperate to the death.

Heading back to the house, we walk close by where the haystack had been. The dirt has taken it; the only signs it once existed are weeds that grow thicker here than elsewhere on the lot. How high the haystack was, how full of the sun, calling me to play—those summer larks. I wonder how many rains, freezes, and thaws it sustained before melting into a dark hump like an oversized grave, before losing even the memory of itself. I tell my grandchildren about sliding down and crawling back up in the unstable straw. My daughter wonders that I didn't suffocate.

Venturing on, we pause at the horse's watering trough, an oil drum sliced in half, drained now and leaning, its wooden frame askew. After Dad sold the horse, he let me keep my turtle collection here. They liked to sun themselves on the algae clumped in the trough's stagnant water. I describe the turtles for my grandchildren: so small they fit in my palm, colored a defiant, deep green, their necks sporting thin red stripes. I thought them as exotic as parrots, and I liked the feel of their tiny claws, the flat, cool underside of their shells in my hand.

Having explored every building on the lot except the grain dryer, which I seldom entered as a child, we've come back full circle to the house. Although, of course, I can't know it now, in two years the contents of the outbuildings will sell at auction—going to private museums, flea-market dealers, farmers from Indiana or Ohio.

We enter the side gate of the yard and decide to check out the wash-house. Chris wants to hear about the baby chicks Mother used to raise, and I show him the room that housed them. Cindy spots what seem to be hundreds of empty apple-juice jars stacked in a corner. I meet Collin's eyes: *No, they never threw away anything.*

Standing in the doorway of the washhouse, my grandchildren ply me with questions about the round concrete structure that's in their view. It's topped with a rusted water tank and sits close to the house. Constructed in my grandparents' day to collect rainwater for the household, the cistern had been abandoned for that use by my parents. They left it, however, to rise, ivy covered, beside the house like the misplaced turret of a castle. Mother and Grandmother Garot had tossed unwanted furniture and bric-a-brac into the cistern's base. As a child, I entered it only once, afraid of its wet, ropy darkness.

At the children's urging, I open the door; the smell of mossy, decades-old humidity assaults me. Chris provides a flashlight, and, despite my admonition about spiders, my grandchildren wade in. Shea exults in finding a Victorian birdcage on a stand, its yellow paint mostly intact. Somehow, it's survived the fate of the objects around it: tables with fractured legs, splayed chairs, metal lawn furniture devastated by rust. I find in a basket the head and body parts of a doll I recognize as mine. I'm dismayed that it has ended here, disassembled by rot and moisture. The boys and Chris solemnly examine these bedraggled castoffs. Chandler, who's becoming an expert forager, draws my attention to some water glasses covered with grime. We had used them every day, although Daddy berated them: "Not big enough to hold a lick of water."

We're on something like an archeological dig into the everyday life of our ancestors. Cindy discovers a wooden tablet with pegs: a vintage grocery-list reminder, probably Grandmother Garot's. I unearth a child's wooden wagon that I recognize as Dad's from an old photograph, and a baseball bat carved with Daddy's initials. My father as a child? It's almost impossible to imagine.

I close the door on our discoveries. I've been advised by my attorney not to remove anything from the premises before the estate is settled. The sounds of a dog barking in the near distance and the *chip-cheep* of sparrows usher me into another time—back to the interloper toad, to rain mingling with dust on the screened porch, to Mother's voice as she reads to me about the cow in the corn. I want to say to my grandchildren, This is where I became who I am. This is the place, the cauldron. But I imagine they see only a crusted yard and a house with dead windows.

I propose we take a tour of the house. We approach the back door from the sidewalk where Nancy and I learned to roller skate, our skates hiccupping over the cracks, Daddy taking movies of us with his new Bell and Howell camera. I battle with the key, and we step into shadows. The electricity's been shut off, and the draperies are drawn, as they always were, against the jangling glare. I've never seen the house this dark in daytime.

All of the contents of the house having been removed to my sister's property, the rooms wait for us like tombs. Merritt holds back, frightened. As the youngest grandchild, he has no consoling memories of this place; to him it must seem macabre. We're all hesitant, facing the ratcheting smell of disuse. As our eyes adjust to the half light, my daughter remarks that it's like "walking through soup."

We've entered the house through the utility room, once home to the washer and dryer. I refrain from telling my grandchildren about the time Mother inadvertently dried a kitten in the dryer, the kitten having climbed into it without her knowledge. This room was the stepchild of the house, the repository of stray vacuum-cleaner parts, lids that fit nothing, and my father's muddy boots. My grandchildren, usually talkative, have fallen silent. When one of them finally speaks, his voice echoes around the walls.

We file into the kitchen. Even without the breakfast table and chairs, it seems small, its counter space measuring no more than three or four feet. I see now why Mother constantly complained of it. Still, it was the soul of the house, where meals were taken, homework done, crises and grievances addressed, and where I watched the family cat one evening playfully torture a captured mouse to death. My father's melee of papers nesting beside the portable radio, the unreliable wall clock, the flyswatter hanging on a nail beside the stove, the stove itself are gone. Only the refrigerator remains, and, realizing Dad's indifferent housekeeping skills, we think better of opening it.

Entering the family room, Charla remarks on the lingering smell of vanilla-scented candles that Mother kept in the closet. I long to see one flickering on the end table. "I used to love the smell of this house," Chris says to me. "Your folks . . . this is just like coming home."

Chris and I well remember Dad's desk, buried alive under stacks of bills and newspapers, his manually operated adding machine home-steading the only cleared spot, the *ka-chunk, ka-chunk* of it as he figures up the payroll, frowning. No one was allowed to dust the desk or move so much as a paper clip from it. The higher the stacks, the more Mother fretted, to no avail. "I know exactly where everything is; just leave it alone," Dad would say. The first and last time I saw the top of the desk was in July of 1955, when Mother did a fearsome cleaning for my wedding reception, held at home.

I want the old sofa back in this room, my mother reading, the afghan of hoyden colors thrown over the sofa's arm. I want to hear the rustling pages of *Woman's Home Companion* as Mother reads, want to hear Fred Allen on the radio. I want to see my sister, five or six years old, riding Flicka, her rocking horse with yellow yarn for a mane and red patent-leather reins. Nancy liked to ride fast; the faster she rode, the louder Flicka's rockers creaked. "Can't you stop that infernal noise?" Dad would demand. My sister would ignore him, rocking into some other world.

"I wonder what became of my doll," Charla muses, glancing at the coat closet where Mother had kept a Madame Alexander doll for her granddaughter's visits. Charla opens the closet, empty except for a few warped hangers. "Do you remember that doll, Mama?" my daughter asks. I do—a sweet-faced beauty whose eyes closed with a polite, almost imperceptible click. We never found her.

"What's going to become of all this," one or the other of us would wonder aloud as we toured the rooms, thinking not only of the house but also of the antique cars, the rotting machinery, the pontifical barn.

We're hailed in the dining room by water stains and a ruined carpet, but they fade as I see Nancy, Mother, Dad, assorted kin, and me gathered around the new Duncan Phyfe table at Thanksgiving, about to partake of baked ham, turkey, Creole gumbo, frozen peaches, and candied sweet potatoes.

Shea and Lauren stare, transfixed, at the wallpaper, with its Southern belles in hoop skirts, carrying parasols. "I wish we dressed like that now," Lauren says.

In the formal living room, the fireplace mantel remains, but not the Venetian-glass pheasants that commanded it, or the ornate, gilded mirror over the mantel in which I checked my lipstick before receiving dates, or the velvet wing chairs in which Mother and Dad sat on Sundays, sharing the *Arkansas Gazette.* The mirror, the chairs, the magisterial birds will end up at closed auction between my sister and me. This was the room so joyous at Christmas: the gas fire glimmering, the expectant gifts, the lopsided tree.

The front door of the house opens into this room. In a piece of sunlight fallen through the door's narrow glass, dust motes come to a rolling boil. Tanner remembers taking a nap here when he was five or six. Waking, his eyes came to rest on the ball-and-claw foot of a Victorian side table. "I started screaming," he says. "I thought some animal was coming to get me. Grandmother hugged me and laughed and said it was only a piece of furniture."

In the adjacent music room, the grand piano still holds court. Almost daily I sat there after school, clumsily practicing scales. Even now, some fifteen years after our visit, Chandler recalls this room and "that huge, black piano."

"The Christmas tree was always in that corner," I tell my grandchildren. They smile politely, but they can't see the tree, skimpy on one side, dripping with silver icicles, crowned with a weary but magical star.

Charla remembers being in this room at Christmas, cajoling her grandfather to bring out his special collection of small, enameled music boxes. After the gifts, after the clean-up of paper and ribbons, Dad would finally produce the exquisite boxes, winding them one by one, releasing a high, thin music. The music inspired a tiny bird inside each box to pop up, twirl, and sing. One of the birds was such a fiery red it seemed to hark back to the first day of birds. Cindy smiles at the memory of this ritual. "Your dad was so much fun," she remarks.

It's getting late. We're losing light, and we still have the upstairs to explore. Merritt is a candidate for adventure now, and he and the other grandchildren charge up the stairs. I follow, remembering the darkness heavy on these steps at bedtime. In winter the bathroom that opened onto the stairway hall was warmed by a gas heater. Snakes and dragons wriggled in its flamelight, cast across the landing's wood floor. Deaf to my mother's protests, Daddy forbade me to touch the light switch, willing me to overcome my fear of the dark. I share this with my daughter. "That's why," I tell her, "I always kept a nightlight on in your room and in Duke's."

We step into my old bedroom, now minus its walnut twin beds and its vanity table with the secret drawer where I kept my diary. Surely it was only a fortnight ago that I lay on the bed in front of a window overlooking the lane, listening to insects rant on the screen, watching a full moon rise, close enough to touch.

We take a quick look at my parents' bedroom, once home to two hand-painted vases Grandmother Garot brought from Belgium, a silver loving-cup won in college by my father, and the forbidden wooden box holding Mother's jewelry. Nothing remains except images crystallizing beyond my reach, invisible to anyone else in the room. Mother and Dad's bedroom had been my refuge as a child, a place to run to when it stormed. The sheen of my mother's satin comforter catches my eye and disappears.

Dusk approaching, we descend the stairs, leaving the attic unexplored. It hasn't been totally emptied, and I long to visit it, but that's for another day. The air has turned soggy and cool. We say our goodbyes and disband, heading home.

Before driving away, I take a long look at the house, the darkening farm lot, the dimming shapes of the fields. In my mind a dust devil, one of many I witnessed here, rises up from the lot, a miniature tornado of energy and despair. I think of the generations of ambitions and egos that clashed here, of the skirmishes of love, jealousy, anger, and desire, played out on the farm as if on Matthew Arnold's "darkling plain."

My children, grandchildren, and I are bound by the land, going back five generations. This place is part of our mutual heritage. Whether our memories of it reach far back or begin today, we share a story—and thereby families are made.

. . . Not much lives on, from one generation
to the next. Not much, but not
nothing.

—SUE KWOCK KIM

The next day, heading back to Pittsburg to resume classes, I realize that I'm guilty of that which, as a child, I deplored in my grandparents. I've regaled my offspring with stories of people and places they haven't seen and can't fully imagine. I've given them, to paraphrase a saying by my friend Miller Williams, nothing they asked and more than they wanted to know.

The family I gathered at the farmhouse couldn't see, of course, the earnest faces of my young parents. They couldn't hear the crooning of the backyard chickens, the smart slam of the screen door, the mongoloid chant of the locusts, rising in the late-light summer yard.

Someday my grandchildren may appreciate the stories I've told them, but now it's unlikely they realize how quickly time devours. By the time they form the questions about their own histories, the people who know the answers likely will be gone. That circle in the ground we shared, however, may one day reappear in the stories they tell, perhaps to their children.

THE OTHER SIDE

My mother dresses chickens.
My father reads.
I call to them.
They glance up, annoyed.

Dad's estate is settled in late 2000, the distribution of property made. I choose the Hot Springs property over the farmhouse and grounds—an excoriating decision. That summer, I make what will be my final visit to the farmhouse before it passes to my sister. On a handsome June day, I bring a photographer friend to record the house and grounds. The house is doggedly slipping away, its roof warping, its columns undermined by rot, the tiles of the veranda chipped, some missing. I find my name and the date, 1940, which my father had scratched in the front sidewalk when it was poured. Another portion of the sidewalk was added in 1948, and Dad put Nancy's name there. Wayward bushes erase the first-story windows. A half-hearted breeze straggles through the trees, immensely taller than they were when I was a child. But not as tall as I remember them.

The photographer takes shot after shot. He poses me sitting on the veranda, standing at the front gate, pausing on the entry steps beside a wasting column. I'm trying to stay the inevitable by recording it, but the house has sided with time. What surprises is how willfully it seems to be fading, not into its past but into its future. Its demeanor has changed, as if it's forgotten me and all it sheltered, as if it's found another purpose now—to join with the dirt and disappear.

CHAPTER 13

Little Diamond and the North Wind

ONCE upon a time there was a boy named little Diamond, the son of a coachman. He slept above a stable of horses, in a bed surrounded by hay. All was well until one winter night a chink fell out of the wall of his room, and the wind found him. Not just any wind—this was the North Wind, an extraordinarily tall, elegant woman with thick, dark, miles-long hair, who invited Diamond to climb into her tresses and ride high over the moonlit world.

"Little Diamond and the North Wind" is an English tale that Mother read to me from *My Bookhouse,* the twelve-volume set of books she'd bought soon after I was born, when money was hard to come by. The legend of the North Wind comes to mind whenever I hear a winter wind bewitching the corners of a house.

Mother kept the volumes of the *Bookhouse* in a secretary with glassed-in bookshelves and three drawers. The shelves held not only *My Bookhouse* but also selections from the Book-of-the-Month Club and assorted curios. Mother crammed the drawers with unlabeled snapshots, last year's Sunday-school lessons, and 1950s pamphlets she'd ordered for me from *Ladies' Home Journal,* with titles such as *Do Boys Like You?* and *How to Be Popular.*

As a child, the poems, stories, and fanciful illustrations in the *Bookhouse* were as real to me as Laddie or my horse-trough turtles. I could easily imagine Diamond's room above the stable—it might have been in our barn loft. It seemed not at all strange to me that the wind could talk. When Mother read that story—I requested it almost every night—I became little Diamond, circling the globe, perched securely on the back of the North Wind. Some alchemy took place in my mind when the wind, which I'd thought invisible, took on a name, a face, and an array of powers. Diamond's North Wind may have underwritten my journey toward becoming a poet.

There were other stories that piqued my imagination. Dame Wiggins of Lee and her seven cats came early into my life, and they've been here ever since—plump and satisfied, in a stoic circle, waiting for milk. The Little Engine That Could, a rusty red, gathers steam even now. The humble and romantic swain, promised a princess for his bride if he could ride his white steed up a mountain of glass, still aims the horse up the impossible incline. And the purple cow ("I'd rather see than be one") retains her foolhardy color to this day.

Mother had her own favorite selections; one featured a teddy bear I soon fell in love with. He was yellow, plump, with a red ribbon around his neck, tied in a bow. He could brush his teeth without help, read a book, and touch his toes. Teddy Bear quite often was the last, lively performer before I crawled into bed.

Teddy Bear, Teddy Bear, go upstairs;
Teddy Bear, Teddy Bear, say your prayers;
Teddy Bear, Teddy Bear, switch off the light;
Teddy Bear, Teddy Bear, say "Good night!"

Under the influence of such rhythm and rhyme, I spent my free time making up stories and conversations, counting out the beats on my fingers. Of course, I had no idea then of prosody, but I reveled in the formal pattern of such nonsense as "Go Ask Your Mother":

Go ask your mother for fifty cents
To see the elephant jump the fence.
He jumped so high, he touched the sky,
And never came down till the Fourth of July.

Daddy's contribution to my love of rhythm and words came in the form of hymns he sang in church, me chiming in beside him. I'd often hear Dad humming them during the week: "How Great Thou Art," "We Gather Together," and "Rock of Ages, Cleft for Me."

Learning to read unfolded as a delight and an obsession. We took our family vacations by car, and I was obnoxious, reading aloud every item along the road: billboards, Burma Shave signs, Welcome! signs for towns, Coca-Cola bottles, the sides of barns. I read from restaurant menus, gum wrappers, cocktail napkins, medicine bottles, and guidebooks. I was expected to write, to keep a daily log of the family's sightseeing; no doubt my parents had promised my teachers to continue my education on these midwinter jaunts. On one memorable trip to California, I recited, sulking and monitored by Dad, my multiplication tables, the twos through the twelves—all across Texas, New Mexico, and Arizona.

Selections in *My Bookhouse* were designed to give pleasure—but not without moral lessons. The themes were handily indexed for parents, including almost every situation imaginable, from "Activity (Industry)," "Crying Instead of Trying," "Loyalty to Mother," "Minding One's Own Affairs," and "Quarrelsomeness," to "Worship, True." It wasn't until I became a parent myself that I knew these groupings existed: as a child, I was lost in the clamor of the stories.

Transferring from *My Bookhouse* in my preteen years to Mother's Book-of-the-Month Club was an uneasy route. I was impressed with those cloth-bound books smelling of ink, their ivory pages thick and deckle-edged. I remember reading, until Mother confiscated it, *The River Road,* by Frances Parkinson Keyes. I liked the heft of this novel, with its dusty-blue cover, marveled at how the ink sank slightly into the paper. To my dismay and surprise, Mother removed the book abruptly from the premises one day: *The River Road* contained words such as "wench" and "bastard," and my mother would have none of this. Nevertheless, I'd discovered writing that took me into the adult world, and I managed to replace, without Mother's knowledge, Ms. Keyes with Frank Yerby.

Reading to me nightly, Mother bequeathed a love of language that led me to writing. Mrs. Miller, my English teachers, Sunday sermons, the radio—all helped lay the groundwork.

The farm also contributed. I had solitude and time and stories to tell while roaming some dirt farm road or another. I experienced the occasional profound silence as the fields, the birds, the rice—the whole universe—turned dumb. There were the sounds of bullbats, mud daubers, a conference of tree frogs. There was the smell of chaff. I was witness to the greening and the dying of grass.

There was no television to watch. I created my own panoply of images, woven from bedtime stories or the violent tales presented in Vacation Bible School or the talk of hired men and preachers.

It was my father, however, who definitively launched my writing career. The first poem I can remember crafting had as its scintillating subjects elves and dew on the grass. When I presented it to my father, he framed it and, with solemn ceremony, placed it on his desk. I was twelve—and from then on an aspiring poet.

I began publishing poems in the mid-1950s and published a poetry chapbook in 1965. This pleased my mother, although she deplored my lack of punctuation and capital letters. (I was an admirer of e. e. cummings in those days.) After I published another chapbook, *Women Who Marry Houses,* Mother called one morning, aflutter. "They're talking about your book on national TV!" she said. They weren't—she'd confused it with a sociological treatise by the same title. I had to tell her they weren't talking about my creation. "Well," Mother said, "it's a good book. I'm proud of you. . . . But why doesn't anything rhyme?"

"What was it like, growing up on a rice farm?" Peter, a visual artist from New York City, asks during one of my MacDowell residencies. "I thought they grew rice only in China," he says, laughing. He pauses. "What *is* a rice farm, anyway?"

We're sitting on the porch of Colony Hall, the colony's central meeting place. It's early evening; we're keeping watch on a nearby meadow, hoping to catch sight of a fox. I tell Peter that life on the farm was hot and dirty and filled with mosquitoes, that my childhood was by turns boring and sensational and reassuring and frightening, like most. I try to explain the sight of levees snaking across a field, of ditches full of yellow bitterweed. I tell him about the diseased green air before a tornado, the song of a red-winged blackbird, the drowning dark of the farm on a moonless night. I say that I didn't have daily access to world-class museums, operas, stage plays, or galleries—those solid advantages of city living. Once a year, only, my family and I might visit such places, pinpointed on vacation itineraries. I tell Peter I was in my mid-twenties before I saw a Picasso that wasn't a calendar print.

When I visit Peter's studio at his invitation the next day, I'm overwhelmed by his paintings—oils depicting lush, bold foliage, simmering with a passion that brings to mind Rousseau. "Where do you see this kind of landscape in New York?" I ask. Peter smiles. "In Central Park. And in my head."

———

"What was it like?" Peter had asked. His question caused me to rethink my life on my father's farm. How, indeed, had that farm shaped me?

Perhaps most important, it granted me, as it had my forebears, a place in the sun. My grandfather Garot had been a rice-growing pioneer, my father had carried on the rice-farming tradition, and my heritage—past, present, and future—lay all around me in my father's fields. I grew up with the Delta sensibility that land is everything.

I felt a pride in how my father made his living. I had the advantage of seeing up close how he spent his working days. I came to realize, also, that the farm was the bond among all my kin. The planting, the droughts, the bountiful times and the bad were the main subjects when the entire family, cousins and all, got together at Thanksgiving and Christmas.

To be a farmer was to be a part of a closed community. Farming—who planted the first rice of the year, who harvested the first field, which tract of land had been lost or sold to whom, whose son would likely follow in his father's farming footsteps and whose wouldn't—was the main subject of conversation and gossip in the local coffee shops. I was a farmer's daughter; by default I belonged to that world, and it gave me a measure of confidence.

There's a lingo that characterizes the world of farming, and those who speak it find it easier to gain entry into the inner circle. Shortly after I began dating Charles, we talked one summer evening about the quick, thin rain that unexpectedly had come up. "It's just a dry shower," Charles observed. "Always happens in July." I hadn't heard the term "dry shower" before, but when I related the conversation to my parents, answering their questions about the evening, Dad nodded approvingly. "Spoken like a true farmer," he said. Although Charles and I dated for another five years, I suspect he was inducted into the family then and there.

The community's favoritism toward farming and ownership of land didn't sit well with some DeWitt residents. More than one shop owner was heard to remark that farmers weren't the only ones to keep long hours or suffer financial setbacks, that they weren't "the only ones on God's green earth." Some grumbled about government subsidies granted farmers, wondering—and, I believe, justly so—where the subsidies for their hardware or grocery or five-and-dime businesses might be.

———

"What was it like?" While life on the farm consisted of mostly halcyon days for me, World War II became a far but palpable presence, like the falls of a distant river. From the time I was six until I was ten, it influenced everything—from the money Daddy made to Mother's hemlines to gas for the car to sugar on the table. Some seventy-odd years later, when somebody mentions war, my first quicksilver thought is of World War II.

With the escalating draft of able-bodied men, the war caused my father endless worry at harvest. No longer able to count on the hoboes or the easy roundup of hands from the woods of Tichnor or Nady, Dad was forced to use German prisoners of war.

I remember the truckload of prisoners who came onto our farm lot one fall day in 1943; I was not quite eight. They arrived standing in an open truck bed, and I remember being surprised at how young they were. I wasn't allowed to go near these men, of course; I wasn't to speak or even nod.

———

There's a distinction, I believe, between dirt and land. Dirt makes one's living; land makes one's heritage. The land holds those who love it as surely as a magnet and as cruelly, sometimes, as an addiction. Why else would an old man, according to a story on National Public Radio, leave the nursing home in his pajamas to walk six winter miles to his ancestral farm, where he was found, frozen? What else can explain the despair of a Grand Prairie farmer who, provisionally turned down for a crop loan and facing foreclosure, hanged himself in the barn? (Minutes after his body was found, a call came from the bank that the loan had been approved.)

In farm families, sons often feel the pull of the land while in their cribs. Duke put in his first crop of rice in a mud puddle, under a willow tree beside the house, when he was four. His grandfather Garot gave him the rice seed; he planted, cultivated, and harvested it, holding a few farmer-to-farmer consultations with his dad. At harvest, after solemn negotiations at the kitchen table, my father bought Duke's crop.

When he was seventeen, Duke grew a bountiful crop of oats on a fifteen-acre field behind our house. It yielded 125–30 bushels per acre. According to George and Bob Carnes, Charles's longtime farming associates, this was the record for oats on the high-producing McDougall farm. Duke remembers that crop as one of the highlights of his farming career, reminiscing that "the field sloped just right for drainage, I got rain when I needed it and a dry spell for harvest, and the ground was good, being an old garden spot. Everything just fell into place."

Like our son, my husband caught the farming bug at an early age. At twelve, he made his first soybean crop, using his dad's machinery. He bought the seed, planted, watered, and harvested the beans. He enlisted assistance with only the cultivating. This was the era before farm machinery sported hydraulic lifts. Since Charles wasn't heavy enough to operate the levers that lifted the cultivator when rounding the turn rows, he was obliged to hire help.

None of my grandchildren grew up on the farms their fathers worked, but the land and the seasons were braided into their days. Wanting to hear their stories, I recently interviewed them, asking what they remembered most about their farming lives.

Collin and Merritt went to the farm with Duke several times a week. Merritt credits seeing the hard work there as forging his work ethic. "I learned," he says, "what would be expected of me in a job, whether or not it was in farming." He absorbed the wisdom of men who work in nature, recalling that during harvest, toward evening, his father always said, "When you see the dust settle just above the ground, it's time to quit." "That's a good thing to live by," Merritt observes.

Collin believes he learned on the farm "the value of doing something with your hands, of producing something tangible," and the satisfaction of "watching people really good at what they do." The farm also provided a jolt of excitement when one day, near the reservoir, he spotted a small black bear.

Tanner and Chandler worked with Chris on his farm until they graduated from high school. "I can't remember when I didn't farm," Chandler says. "I learned, from being responsible for the rice—watering, walking the levees—how to handle things on my own." He recollects the day he went into a flooded rice field "barefoot, without a shovel," and was chased out of the field by a cottonmouth.

Tanner relates that "farming taught me how to be a worker, how to get up in the morning and get going. It's part of me I'll never lose." He recalls the anticipation of "something new every day—maybe a deer in the field or a bird that's angry because you're there." He adds, "I loved the smell of the dirt being turned in the spring. I wish my son could have the experience. . . . I'd love to put him on a tractor."

Chris raised corn and cotton as well as rice, and both Shea and Lauren remember playing in the loaded cotton cart, "making tunnels." Shea remembers eating corn "right out of the field" and walking barefoot in the mud of the farm, "making mud shoes." Lauren liked "picking cattails out of the ditch" and "flagging for the cropduster." All the grandchildren credit time on the farm for having given them a chance to bond with their fathers.

Although my husband, son, and son-in-law—each having farmed for over twenty-five years—left farming to pursue other careers, they can't, they report, entirely shake its hold. They speak of the pangs of loss that strike like incoming artillery at the smell of wet dirt at planting time or the first singeing air of harvest. They agree that each misses being his own boss. Charles says that what he misses most is "the feeling—erroneous, of course—that you're the master of your universe."

And what do I myself miss? Fields, water-covered fields—at sunset, the color of abalone shell; by moonlight, pages of steel.

My husband's land has passed out of the family, as has the farmland

Nancy and I inherited, except for the acreage lying partially along Thompson Cemetery Road near DeWitt, which Dad referred to as the north farm. I've retained this; it's rented, planted in rice and soybeans, and my grandsons go there to fish and hunt. The Stone farms remain in Chris's family. Nancy has kept the grounds on which the Garot farmhouse, barn, and outbuildings sit. She and I remain estranged.

The McDougall farm, lost to us in the mid-1980s, was sold at auction in Stuttgart from the courthouse steps. The buyer, respecting Duke's track record in farming, invited him to farm it. Thus, in a quirk of fate, Duke rented the land that had belonged to his father. He also rented the acreage belonging to his uncle Jim Spicer, now deceased. (The son of rice historian J. M. Spicer, Jim was our brother-in-law.) Duke, Cindy, Collin, and Merritt were named North Arkansas County's outstanding farm family in 1994, echoing the honor given Duke's grandparents Garot over thirty years before.

Living with melanoma for over thirteen years, Charla died in 1999. She was forty-one. She raised her children into their teens but saw only Tanner graduate from high school. Honoring her request, we buried her in Flat Bayou Cemetery, which lies near Chris's ancestral land in Jefferson County, near Wabbaseka. Influenced early in life by reading Rachel Carson's *Silent Spring,* Charla wanted in death to be under the shade of the ancient oaks of that cemetery, amidst the sounds she'd grown up with—crickets, mockingbirds, and owls. In spring, when tractors work the nearby fields, veils of diesel smoke drift near her grave.

In the what-we're-doing-now department, Lauren, Shea, and Chandler are married, with children, working in cities but choosing to reside in rural areas or small towns. Chris works in Little Rock as a plant operator for Novus, a corporation specializing in food additives for livestock. He lives in the country, between Wabbbaseka and Altheimer, raising an enviable garden every year.

Duke and Cindy, divorced, have each remarried. Duke is the draftsman for Stuttgart's municipal waterworks; his wife, Lori, is senior accounts-payable clerk for Producers Rice Mill. They live in Stuttgart, a primarily agricultural town. Collin recently obtained a degree in transportation and logistics from the University of Arkansas; Merritt will soon graduate from the university's school of engineering.

Charles and I live in the metropolitan area of Kansas City. Just outside the city limits lie fields of wheat; I am never far from fields. Charles works as a commercial real estate appraiser, and I continue to write poetry. It still doesn't rhyme.

In the family now are teachers, caregivers, a sales representative, a transportation manager, a welder, an administrator, a truck driver, a speech pathology major, daycare providers, an equipment-utilization coordinator, a brazer, a creative designer, a biochemical engineering student, a store manager, a student barber, a patient-coordinator, and clerks. There are no farmers.

———

DeWitt, 158 years old at this writing, remains a constant in my life. Although smaller than in its agricultural heyday, it thrives. I'm happy to see the courthouse of my youth still standing, the traffic, as always, channeled one way around the square. The library long ago moved into its own lodgings. Gallery G remains, owned by Nancy. Gay Hudspeth's house is gone. There's a new bypass, high school, and jail. The congregation of First United Methodist built a new church on DeWitt's outskirts, bringing to it the stained-glass windows my grandfather Garot, the Lepine family, and others had given. The old church is now a shelter for abused children. The building that housed Scougale's Jewelers, scheduled for renovation, will hold a pub. The aquifer under the Grand Prairie, seen by the early rice farmers as an endless lake, has all but disappeared. The *DeWitt Era Enterprise* still reports on the town, and many of the old family names I knew remain in the phone book.

The north farm provides my tie to the farming world. It remains reassuringly there, ever and never changing.

———

Of course it saddens me that most of Daddy's land and the McDougall land is now out of the family. That's not the way Charles and I envisioned the future fifty-five years ago when we married and were raising our children on the McDougall farm, visiting Dad and Mother on theirs, expecting one day to pass the land down to our progeny. Mother's admonition to "love and cherish this home and farm" haunts me to this day; clearly she and Daddy expected that the Garot land would stay in the family.

Things change, however, and we adapt—a lesson in resilience the land itself teaches, even as it brings us loss. As a Texan rancher friend says, "You can love the land, but it doesn't always love you back."

Nevertheless, to have realized one's dream, even if only for a short while, is an accomplishment. A farmer is by nature an optimist: losing one dream, he'll seek another. And, though he may lose farming, he has not lost everything. The stories and the memories remain.

In his essay "Lucky Man," published in the *New Yorker,* drama critic John Lahr discusses one of the late playwright Horton Foote's most famous characters, Carrie Watts. In *The Trip to Bountiful,* the aging Watts finally realizes her dream of escaping her son's city apartment for a last visit to the land. She tells her son, when he comes to take her back to the city, "Pretty soon it'll all be gone . . . this house . . . me . . . you. . . . But the river will be here. The fields. The woods. . . . We're part of all this. We left it, but we can never lose what it has given us."

Tellingly, Lahr notes that Watts "finds salvation not, as expected, in the land but in the journey."

Much of my past has drifted away, but some touchstones remain—a color-tinted photograph of the Garot farmhouse as it was in 1910, a Waterford chandelier, the grandfather clock, a quilt, a ceramic cat. Rice stalks from a crop Duke made on the McDougall farm reside next to my desk.

These icons remind me: the small civilizations of my kin are toppled and gone; yet they did live. By memory's generosity, they still do.

I find that every horse is Daisy, every fedora my father's, every teddy bear the *Bookhouse* bear, who nightly said his prayers. In a nanosecond the past and the present brush, moving on.

Afterword

HAVING set down the legends of a farm, a time, and my kin in this tribute to them, I know better now who my vanished predecessors were, the complex worlds they inhabited, the subtle ways they shaped me. I understand more completely my parents' obsession with hanging onto things, hoping to keep the past alive. I've answered many of the questions with which I began my journey into the lives of my forebears—although I haven't yet found who among them wore a Confederate uniform.

I think it amazing that, as young children, we don't question our surroundings. They are what they are, and we are set down in them like characters on a stage, in medias res. We don't judge or evaluate. We listen; we learn our lines. Only later, as experience makes us more keen, do we try to make sense of that tangled, dense copse of childhood.

I was lucky: my parents, grandparents, and the whole vivid, extended tribe provided a tableau against the dark, shielding me from it, taking me into their bright worlds.

Indeed, I found my way in this world alongside a compelling array of kin, and they proved to be sparkling companions. Over time, as with a painting left in the sun, their colors and outlines have faded, rumors of shapes where shapes had been. For me, however, they live in their fully faceted dimensions, no farther than my remembering.

Reflecting on my childhood, I realize that the onerous task of decapitating a chicken has seen me through many a challenge. If I can do that, I remind myself, I can do anything.

I'm grateful for the solidarity of my hometown, for the folk of DeWitt, who plied their trades in steadfast faith, who believed in and watched over me. They've edged themselves, in various guises, into my work.

And I'm grateful for Daddy's money. It caused a regrettable rift in the family, yet it gave me a true childhood. It provided me time, space, and the freedom to be, whenever I wished, little Diamond—secure in the tresses of the North Wind, rising with her, high above the farm.

Works Cited

Allen, Garner. "Justice Coming Home." *Grand Prairie Historical Society Bulletin* (April 2003).

"Arkansas County Court House." *Arkansas Ties.* http://www.arkansasties.com.

"Davy Crockett." In *The Encyclopedia of Arkansas History and Culture,* ed. Jeff Bailey. May 19, 2008. http://www.encyclopediaofarkansas.net.

"DeWitt (Arkansas County)." In *The Encyclopedia of Arkansas History and Culture,* ed. C. F. Scott. February 25, 2010. http://www.encyclopediaofarkansas.net.

DeWitt: A 150 Year Journey. DeWitt, AR: DeWitt Era-Enterprise, 2003.

Kim, Sue Kwock. "Translations from the Mother Tongue." *New England Review* 21.1 (2000): 76–77.

Lahr, John. "Lucky Man: Horton Foote's Three Acts." *New Yorker,* October 26, 2009, 88–93.

Spicer, J. M. *Beginnings of the Rice Industry in Arkansas.* Stuttgart, AR: Arkansas Rice Promotion Association, 1964.